Lessons
OUT OF THE
Body

Also by Robert S. Peterson

Out of Body Experiences

Lessons
Out of the Body

*A Journal of Spiritual Growth
and Out-of-Body Travel*

Robert Peterson

HAMPTON ROADS
PUBLISHING COMPANY, INC.

Cover painting by Louis Jones
titled "Neptune's Daughter"
Cover design by Marjoram Productions

For information, write:

Hampton Roads Publishing Co., Inc.
1125 Stoney Ridge Road
Charlottesville, VA 22902

434-296-2772
fax: 434-296-5096
e-mail: hrpc@hrpub.com
www.hrpub.com

If this book is unavailable from your local bookseller,
it may be obtained directly from the publisher.
Call toll-free 1-800-766-8009 (orders only).

Library of Congress Catalog Card Number: 2001094008

ISBN 1-57174-251-4

10 9 8 7 6 5 4 3 2 1

Printed on acid-free paper in Canada

CREDITS

I gratefully acknowledge permission to reprint portions of the following material:

Anderson, Jon. *Horizon* Copyright, 1983, Spheric B.V./Warner Bros. Music, from the Polydor Ltd. Jon and Vangelis album, *Private Collection*. Quotation used with permission.

Gabbard, Glen O., Twemlow, Stuart W. *With the Eyes of the Mind: An Empirical Analysis of Out-of-Body States* Praeger Publishers, New York, NY., 1984. Portions reprinted with permission.

Grosso, Michael. *The Parapsychology of God* appears as chapter 5 of the book *Body Mind Spirit* Hampton Roads Publishing, 1997. Portions used with permission.

Mack, John E. *Abduction* Ballantine Books, New York, NY., 1994. Portions reprinted with permission.

O'Neill, Paul. *Edge of Thorns* Copyright, 1993, MCA Music Corporation, from the Atlantic Records Savatage album, *Edge of Thorns*. Quotation used with permission.

Scholz, Tom. *My Destination* Copyright, 1986, Hideaway Hits, from the MCA Records Boston album, *Third Stage*. Quotation used with permission.

TABLE OF CONTENTS

ACKNOWLEDGMENTS

I'd like to thank the following people for their support:

My wife, Kathy, whose love and encouragement kept me flying high, and whose wholesomeness kept me centered and grounded.

My mom, who made me who I am today. She taught me to believe in myself, and in God. She taught me that I should love and have faith in myself, in God, and in others. She taught me to reach for the stars, set my sights high and never give up my dreams. She taught me that we can do anything we set our minds to, and that we should not let anything come between us and our goals.

Julia Jablonski for her outstanding editing work and suggestions.

Those who have inspired me with their music: Paul O'Neill, Jon Oliva, and the bands Savatage, Trans-Siberian Orchestra, Stratovarius, and Dream Theater.

PART ONE

LIFE LESSONS

THE NEXT STEP

Glide on silver wings of air,
Float on top of mountain breezes,
Reach up for the highest good,
Lift your spirit higher than the farthest reaches of
*   space,*
Pour your soul into the ocean of Love,
For Love is the most sacred accomplishment.
To this end, will we all one day meet.
                                                    —Inner Voice

On September 9, 1979, I read the book *Journeys Out of the Body* by Robert Monroe. It was a book that changed my life forever. Instantly, I became fascinated with the possibility that we could somehow learn to leave our bodies and step into a different reality, transcending the limitations of the flesh. Most of the books called this astral projection, out-of-body experiences, or OBEs. Up to that point, I was skeptical and science-oriented. Everything Monroe said went against all of my religious and scientific beliefs, but Monroe explained astral projection in such a logical and scientific manner that it appealed to me right away. Instead of asking readers to believe his assertions, he asked them to try it for themselves. Monroe even gave a technique to induce OBEs in his book. I decided to try Monroe's method, mainly out of curiosity.

Much to my surprise, Monroe's method gave me immediate results: I had a terrifying run-in with "the vibrations,"[1] a convincingly real precursor to an out-of-body experience. From that point on, I was hooked; I had to explore it further. Had it not been for that instant gratification, I would probably have lost interest in OBEs and gone back to living my shallow, mundane, and materialistic life. Instead, Monroe's book started me on a high-speed roller-coaster ride of out-of-body experiences and psychic powers.

My mom and dad instilled in me a firm belief that I could achieve any goal if I had enough willpower, focus, and determination to learn the necessary skills. Though I've always set high expectations for myself, I've also always had the determination of a barracuda. For example, I once took a community education class to learn woodworking. When the instructor asked me to pick out my very first woodworking project, I didn't ask him for suggestions. Instead, I told him I was going to build a grandfather clock. Somehow he managed to keep from laughing, and kindly suggested that I try something simpler. To appease him, I built a simple

---

[1] Many people feel "vibrations" before or after an out-of-body experience. These vibrations range from very mild sensations, such as buzzing or tingling, to very intense sensations, where it feels like electricity is running through the body. This is often accompanied by sounds, ranging from a very mild humming to a very intense roaring.

wooden box that was done in one week, but my second project was, in fact, a grandfather clock, and I built it entirely from plans and planks of wood, not from a kit.

So after I finished reading Monroe's book, I had the same determination to learn how to induce out-of-body experiences. I began meditating, studying, and inducing altered states of consciousness, including OBEs. Although I only wanted to have OBEs, I got an unexpected by-product: I started having weird psychic experiences of every kind. Often the coincidences and synchronicities in my life piled up to the point of absurdity, to the point where I could no longer deny that psychic experiences were real or that they were happening to me. I also discovered how to communicate with an inner source of wisdom I call my "inner voice." I don't know exactly what my inner voice is, but I'm sure that everyone has one. Some people may call it their "spirit guide," but I don't think it's all that complex or mysterious; I think it's just a link from my conscious self to my "higher self" via my subconscious. Fortunately for me, I documented almost all of my unusual experiences in several journals. (I highly recommend journal writing, not only as a means of documenting your experiences, but also to help you organize, remember, and focus your spiritual life.)

My out-of-body adventures were many and varied. After studying and practicing OBEs for more than ten years, I had amassed a collection of books containing almost every volume on the subject of OBEs. After having read all but a few, I felt that there were a lot of misunderstandings and superstitions about the subject. For example, many of the OBE books approached the subject from an occult point of view, treating astral projection as some sort of psychic paranormal power, despite the fact that most OBEs happen to normal, ordinary people. Gabbard and Twemlow, in their 1984 book *With the Eyes of the Mind,* point out "the 'typical' profile of the OBE subject is remarkably similar to the average, healthy American individual. The individual may be of any age and is equally likely to be male or female" (p. 40). I believe there's no such thing as a paranormal experience. No one out there is breaking the laws of physics. I think it's more correct to say that our knowledge of the laws of physics is incomplete, since those laws don't leave room for the experiences we label "paranormal," such as OBEs.

I also discovered that most OBE books are sketchy at best when it comes to giving directions on how to induce an out-of-body experience. Some of the OBE books seemed like glorified storytelling. Without providing any methodology, the readers were left on their own to believe or not and only wishing they could do it themselves. Other books provided methods, but very vague ones.

I don't think those authors were deliberately trying to hide their knowledge. It's more likely that most OBE adepts are either right-brained, artistic people, or naturally gifted people. The artistic ones have probably never analyzed what they do to induce their OBEs. The naturally gifted ones just slip into that state, so it's nearly impossible for them to describe what they do to get there. Usually, their instructions looked something like this:

1. Relax totally.
2. Imagine floating.
3. Now that you're out of your body, go ahead and explore.

Unlike those artistic or natural projectors, I'm a computer programmer, an analytical thinker. Most of my early OBE years were spent just experimenting and analyzing what works and what doesn't. I was like a first-time golfer who makes only one good swing during his game, then stops to ask himself what he did differently from all his other miserably botched swings earlier in the game. There was a lot of trial and error.

In the early years, I spent more time examining the *process* of leaving the body and how to do it than actually exploring the out-of-body state itself. Many times, I was so focused on learning the induction process that I decided to forgo experimentation so that I could study the process of leaving and reentering the body. A fitting analogy is when someone trains to become a pilot; he or she develops the necessary skills by repeatedly taking off and immediately landing again.

I finally realized that I had to write my own book to clear up some basic misunderstandings and present some concrete methods of inducing out-of-body experiences. My first book was *Out of Body Experiences: How to Have Them and What to Expect*, published in 1997.

I'm sure that nearly every writer goes through the same thing I went through next. As soon as I submitted the text for publication, I needed to reread and reproof the text several times for errors. In the process, I thought of all the things I forgot to say in the first book. Over and over again, I'd kick myself for some omission. For example, why hadn't I addressed the issue of psychic protection? Plus there were all the new things I'd learned during the two-year publication process.

Then one day in July of 1997, I was looking at a copy of my newly released book. At first I was pleased to see the outcome of so many hours of work, but looking through my book, I had to stop and ask myself, "Where's the spirituality?" Out-of-body experiences gave me the most important aspect of my spirituality: a certain nonphysical perspective on life and its lessons. If not for the lessons, there would be no point in coming to this earthly life. I had many lessons, both in the body and out. In the first book, I mentioned in passing that OBEs made me a more spiritual person, but I was reluctant to put much spirituality (in the form of lessons) into the book. I tried to keep the book as down-to-earth as possible. I wrote about the simple out-of-body experiments I did: exploring the different types of astral eyesight, my attempts at learning to fly, getting into my body backward, and so on. Now I felt the weight of that decision on my shoulders. My inner voice piped up: "So *do* something about it! Write another book!" "Come on," I retorted. "What would I write about? The invisible helpers who take hold of my hands and cart me off to faraway places? Who cares?" "Write about what you've learned."

I wasn't convinced. I wasn't sure I wanted to write another book. First, I certainly didn't care about the money. At that time, I hadn't seen any money from the sales of my book, and I didn't expect to make much money from royalties. Just after the book was published, I met and spoke with William Buhlman, author of *Adventures beyond the Body,* an excellent book that was published after my text was submitted for publication. Buhlman told me frankly that I'd starve if I relied on book sales to pay the bills. People don't write OBE books to make money, because there isn't a large enough target audience. Besides, if I had cared about the money, I wouldn't have offered the entire text of my book *absolutely free* on the Internet two years before the book's final publication.

I wasn't looking for fame either. I was (and am) a private, introverted person. If anything, I was deathly afraid of the public's reaction to my book. I still hadn't told my mom, my sister, my wife's relatives, or any of my friends that I had written a book on such an off-the-wall topic, and I was dreading the day I'd have to talk about it with them. How would my boss react? I tried to push thoughts like these out of my mind, telling myself not to worry. The book had been a labor of love.

The hardest part about writing the first book was coming up with a title. "What is the title of my next book?" I asked my inner voice playfully, expecting not to get an answer. As soon as I formulated the question, my inner voice responded with *"Flying with Angels,"* and at that point, I knew it wasn't joking.

Soon after *Out of Body Experiences: How to Have Them and What to Expect* was released, I started getting e-mail from people who had read the book. Many of them noticed that the book contained experiences mostly from my early years of astral projection, and they wanted to know what I've been doing since those early experiences, what else I've learned, and where it's taken me.

So what have my OBEs taught me? How have they made me more spiritual? What have I done with them besides the simple experiments? What have I encountered on the journey and, more importantly, what lessons have I learned? That is the subject of this new book.

Professor Charles Tart, the famous OBE researcher who did laboratory experiments on Robert Monroe and other OBE experiencers, once wrote:

I'm very impressed by the two answers regarding the purpose of life given by people who have had near-death experiences. From their physical rendezvous with death, the most common answer they give is that the purpose of life is to learn how to love. The second most common answer they give is that the purpose of life is to contribute to human knowledge (Tart 1994).

My entire life has been an affirmation of Professor Tart's statement. I've had many life-lessons, and most of them concerned the subject of love. Some lessons were learned through normal in-the-body experiences. Others were facilitated by out-of-body experiences. Many times, I learned these lessons through a combination of the two.

This book is divided into two parts. Part 1 is about the spiritual lessons I've learned, both in the body and out of it. Part 2 is educational, with out-of-body information and techniques for people who want to have their own OBEs.

2

PERSPECTIVE

A fly wanders back and forth through the air,
   then lands on the windowpane.
It launches itself, flies for two feet, then lands on
   the glass again.
It continues to walk around, on the glass, never
   finding the exit.
It doesn't know that there is an opening in the
   window just a few feet away.
You and I can see the opening because we have
   the bigger picture.
If only the fly would unlimit itself, get the bigger
   picture,
and allow itself the freedom and perspective to fly
   higher,
it could rise above it all and be free.
Instead, it is content to wander aimlessly.
Now I tell you: You are that fly. You know the
   way out.
But you choose to ignore it.

                                    —Inner Voice

My story begins when I was going to the University of Minnesota from 1980 to 1984. It was a time when I was truly happy. My life was not quite as complicated as it is today.

The best times of all were spring and summer (Minnesota winters can be harsh). My best friends in the world were John (at school), LD (at work), and my brother Joe and his wife, Candy. I worked for the Minnesota Department of Natural Resources then, doing computer programming odd jobs.

My early out-of-body experiences taught me that the physical world was superficial, a façade covering the "real" world. I was introverted, so I didn't feel the need to share my experiences with anyone, and I was afraid of the reaction I'd get if I ever did.

I didn't own a car or motorcycle, so I got around mostly by bus or bicycle. I used to spend hours waiting for buses, hours riding on buses, and hours waiting between my classes, so there was always plenty of time for introspection back then. I used that time for development of the psyche: psychic development. At times I was very psychically sensitive. How psychic I was changed from week to week, depending on the meditation/OBE exercises I was doing and how much of my time was taken up by college.

I loved to take long walks and listen to my inner voice. Sometimes it automatically spoke to me as I walked. Other times I would start the conversation by asking, "What is love?" or "What's today's lesson?" and every time I would get a different response, like "Love is the anchor-bolt of the universe." Once I started this inner dialogue, it was easy to maintain the connection. I found that if we take the time to listen to that inner voice deep inside us all, it can teach us things we never dreamed of.

I remember walking around campus with a backpack full of books. Instead of my class books, I had books on spirituality, OBEs, religion, philosophy, psychology, even sociology. I remember finding obscure places on campus to read, like in the basement hallway of Northrop Auditorium. People would walk past me and not say a word. If they could have read my mind, they would have been overwhelmed by the joy inside me, radiating out in all directions. I never wanted to read in one place for too long. After reading for a half-hour, I would have to move to another place. It was almost as if the room had filled with joy, and couldn't hold any more.

I was an introvert back then. I felt like some kind of freak because weird things were happening to me on a daily basis. No one else around me was having psychic experiences and out-of-body experiences, and when I tried to talk about them, it made people too uncomfortable. It seemed like there was no one I could talk to. Sometimes I would go outside and watch the beautiful college girls walk by the buildings. There were thousands of girls, all of them to me beautiful beyond words. Some were beautiful on the outside, and some were beautiful on the inside—I could feel it psychically. I remember thinking: "There are so many beautiful people. Each is unique. Each has a whole world inside them. How can I pick just one of them as my mate?" At the same time it seemed impossible to find a mate who could begin to understand me; she'd have to be as weird as I was.

I always thought about how grand it would be if I could spend a whole lifetime exploring each and every human being that I met, both men and women. I thought that if I worked hard and developed my psychic abilities well enough, I could learn to explore their minds with my mind.

Not only did I want to "explore" everybody, I also wanted to show everybody who I was, too. I saw so many miserable people on the streets and on the buses, and I wanted to tell them how wonderful life could be. I wanted to tell them that happiness doesn't depend on what physical objects you own, where you live, or even what you're doing. Happiness is what you feel inside, and each of us can *choose* to feel happy any time—all the time! No one has to be sad, no matter how bad things seem.

We could view each experience as a learning experience. We could choose to see the love, goodness, and truth in the world, in each living thing. We could learn to see ourselves in others and to see others in ourselves. We could learn to accept ourselves for who we are right now, and choose a straight path into the future to the best "us" we can be. We could learn to accept others as they are right now, love them right now, and know we are only seeing a small snapshot of that person in time. We can see their potential for spiritual growth over time. We can also see God because I believe that God is inside each of us. All we need to do is let God out: Show people! Get in touch with the God inside you!

When you view the physical world from an out-of-body perspective, you start to realize that this world is just a playground for spiritual growth and that we're all just "passing through" this place as part of a much larger journey. Trivial things start to take the back seat. Even important things start to take the back seat. What's left in the front seat? Joy. Love. Happiness. Tears. Emotions. Experiences. Laughter. Life. Then you can start to see life as a journey, and not as a predicament. You can view each experience, good and bad, as a steppingstone to a greater you. And as God works through us, our lessons are given to us like clockwork. Sometimes they're handed to us on a silver platter. Other times they're thrown, like pies, in our faces.

3

THE WOLF'S LESSON

"What's today's lesson?" I asked my inner voice.
"All creatures are creatures of God."

One of my early lessons came on the morning of May 31, 1982. I only had seventy-four out-of-body experiences to my credit, so I was still a little afraid of them. This lesson was about fear, and it took the form of a dream.

I was trying to induce an OBE, but I fell asleep instead. In my dream, I was near my Minneapolis home, walking toward the back door. Oblivious, I had passed by four dark objects, and now I turned to see what they were. What I saw stopped me in my tracks. The objects were the biggest, blackest, meanest wolves I had ever seen. At first the wolves were calm, but now they could sense my fear, and my fear convinced them of their superior position. The wolves reacted instantly, lunging toward me with their white fangs bared and hate burning in their eyes. Terrified, I raced to the screen door of the porch and darted inside. The wolves were still snapping and growling on the other side of the door as I stood on the porch and pondered my situation.

After a long time, the wolves calmed down. Then I heard my brother coming home. He saw one of the wolves and he mistook it for a big black dog. He patted it on the head and started walking to the porch. The wolf growled, and I told my brother to hurry, that they were vicious wolves. He ran to the door and the wolves attacked him, but he made it inside safely. After a while, the wolves went away and timidly we ventured outside. In a few minutes, the wolves came back and attacked again, but I was ready for them and dashed inside again. As before, I barely managed to escape their bloodthirsty jaws.

Again, I waited for the wolves to leave, then I cautiously went outside again. When I was distracted, the wolves came back. This time, one of the wolves cleverly got behind me and blocked my way to the door that had been my safe haven. I looked back at the wolf that blocked the way to the door. I knew for certain that I couldn't retreat. The wolves circled me, growling, planning how best to devour me. I looked into the eyes of two wolves, reading them, judging them. I could see the hate in their eyes and I knew they wanted to kill me, but I sensed now that something was holding them back.

Then I looked at the wolf closest to me. It was a female, and much bigger than the others. She was the alpha of the pack, and she kept the others at bay. The huge female wolf looked at me with a terrible, fierce look in her eyes. She raised her left paw toward me, as if asking me to make the next move.

I looked deeply into her eyes, and my mind reached out to hers. When my mind touched the she-wolf's mind, I felt a kind of empathy. Impulsively, I stooped over and took hold of her paw with both of my hands. Upon touching her, I was flooded with emotions. My fear was overwhelmed by a deep under-standing of the wolves, and I was filled with a powerful love. This was not a personal love, but a deep love of great friendship.

As my love reached out for this wolf, I could feel the wolf's love returning to me. The emotions I felt were indescribable. I got down on all fours and I embraced the black wolf the way wolves do. I stood up on my knees and the wolf stood up on her hind paws and we embraced again, this time in the manner of humans: we hugged. Then I got a telepathic message from her. She told me that as long as I was the wolf's friend, her peers would never harm me. I knew I would be her friend for life. The dream ended there.

I had hoped to induce an OBE that morning to learn more about the out-of-body state. What I got instead was a dream that had a lot of hidden messages. My inner voice helped me to interpret them:

• Giving in to fear is giving up control.

• Fear feeds on itself. Being fearless dispels danger.

• If you try to run away from fear, it always comes back.

• The key to conquering fear is to understand it. Understand its motivations and mechanisms.

• The only solution to fear is to face it, embrace it, and love it. Love can overcome it.

• Once conquered, your greatest fears can become your greatest allies.

- Reach out your mind to others, and you may discover that we are all creatures of God.

- If you send out your love unselfishly, it always returns in some form.

In our modern society, we are often taught to disregard dreams as meaningless subconscious garbage, but this dream was more than that. This dream reminded me of stories I had read about Native Americans seeking spiritual guidance through a solitary journey they call a "vision quest." Were the wolves real astral beings sent to teach me a life-lesson? Perhaps. The messages were important regardless of the source.

4

MEETING WITH A MASTER

*"What's today's lesson?" I asked my inner voice.
"Today, remind yourself occasionally that this world,
what you see, hear, taste, smell, and feel, is all an
illusion."*

On Friday, August 13, 1982, I had a powerful experience. It was so incredible that, even after I had eighty OBEs under my belt, I denied its reality, calling it a lucid dream in my journal. Years later, I had reason to believe it was an OBE.[2]

At first I was dreaming peacefully that I was standing near the two-story house where I grew up in Minneapolis. On the boulevard was our huge elm tree. I looked down at the sidewalk and suddenly it occurred to me, "Hey! This is a dream!" With that I was fully conscious and lucid.

---

[2]Unless you've had both lucid dreams and OBEs and seen the transition from one to the other, it's hard to tell the difference. See chapter 25 for a detailed examination of this subject.

I wasted no time. I took a leap to fly, but I fell flat on my face in the middle of the street. I picked myself up a bit, without standing up. I wondered if what I was experiencing was real or imaginary. Usually if it's a dream, I can fly without problems. I can fly in OBEs too, but I wasn't very good at it. I thought to myself, "The book[3] was absolutely right. You don't consciously question reality like this in a dream." I was excited about the experience, but I wondered why I couldn't fly. I stood up, walked back, and tried again. I fell again. I walked back yet again. I figured the problem must be in my mind.

"This time," I thought, "I'll find out for sure if this is an OBE or a lucid dream." I took the third flying leap. This time I paid attention to how the falling felt. For a second or two I was weightless. I couldn't feel gravity. I could tell that I was most likely being pulled to the ground because of my beliefs rather than from gravity. I found myself flat on my face once again, but this time I picked myself up and thought, "Aha! I bet if I try hard enough, I can fly." I tried a couple more times, each from different locations and each without success.

I thought to myself that my problem with flight had something to do with being insecure and lacking confidence, but what could I do to build my confidence? I decided to cross the street and try again, but I saw two cars coming down the street from opposite directions. I thought to myself, "If I'm out of my body, cars can't hurt me. Maybe this is my opportunity to build my confidence." I walked out into the middle of

---

[3] The fiction book I was reading at the time was *The House between the Worlds* by Marion Zimmer Bradley.

the street. The cars passed by me, one on each side of me. After the cars had passed, I tried to fly again, but that attempt was also unsuccessful.

Without warning, my consciousness blurred, but it wasn't long before I became conscious again. I was still standing in the street near my house, but now I saw people around me, all about my age. The people were milling about, experimenting like I always did during my OBEs. Some of them were talking. I got the impression they were preparing for something.

Then I looked to my right and saw "Him." It was "the master." He looked about forty years old, and my first impression was that he could very well be a friend or mentor of Don Juan Matus, of whom Carlos Castaneda wrote. My memory opened up and I realized that I knew this master. I knew I had seen him before, although I couldn't pin down when or where. I remembered seeing him lift a fully grown man with one hand, palm open, over his head as a demonstration of his power.

Even though it seemed incredible, I knew he was *my* master. I was one of his many students and apprentices, as were all the people who were crowded around me in the street. The other students formed a circle around the master and they were asking him questions. I realized that the other students were just like me, learning to become more spiritual. Like me, most of them were at the stage where they were learning to master out-of-body travel.

I wanted to ask him why I had trouble flying, but I didn't want to be rude and push my way to the front. Patiently, I waited for the crowd to thin out. Finally, when most of the students had left, I approached the master and asked, "Master, why can't I fly when I astrally project?" Although he did not look Oriental, he reminded me of a Chinese martial arts master because his words were very concise, wise, and meaningful. They had hidden meanings. In fewer words than I can say it, he told me my problem with flying was within my mind, that practice would clear it up, and that next time I had an OBE, he would try to help me mentally.

Remembering his superhuman strength, I asked him, "Master, I've seen you pick up a man with one hand. Is the power you harness to do this called chi?"[4] He answered me with a parable:

> There was once a farmer.
> One day he went out to his field and dug up a potato.
> Later, he dug up three apples.
> Later still, he dug up three oranges.
> But his field was not a potato field.
> Neither was it a field of apples, nor of oranges.

I was completely conscious when he told me this. In the same manner as before, I got multiple meanings from his statement:

- The farmer's "field" is like a person's "field of energy."

- The content of something (i.e., the field) does not necessarily make up that something. We are more than we think we are.

---

[4]*Chi* or *Qi* is the metaphysical energy cultivated in martial arts, through exercises like T'ai Chi Ch'uan and Qigong.

- Many different "fruits" can be harnessed from a field of power. We have unbelievable potential for power and spirituality, if we learn the key.

As I left the master, a fellow student came up to me and said, "Come on. There's something you should see." My consciousness blurred again. The next thing I knew, the student and I were at the top of a church steeple. I looked down and had an instinctual fear reaction. This was not a small church. I'd been to the top of the Notre Dame Cathedral, and this was much higher. I thought, "Oh my God, what if I fell from here?" Then my inner voice said, "There is your test." I knew exactly what it meant: some day I would have to face a big test of spiritual confidence by falling from that height, depending on my flight to save me. After that I lost consciousness.

Years later, in September 1985, I described this experience to a group of friends in Phoenix. One of the guys said that he had had the same experience, exactly as I described. Although he lived in Phoenix at the time, he described standing in the street with a crowd of students, next to a large tree. He said there were two- or three-story houses nearby. He described learning to fly, and a master figure that wasn't Oriental, but had an Oriental persona. He didn't remember exactly when his experience occurred, but he said it might have been the same general time frame as mine.

This experience taught me that there *are* masters out there who help astral travelers. I learned that I wasn't alone; I was one of many students in the same path. I also learned that a greater test of my confidence was yet to come.

5

ASTRAL LYNCH MOBS

"What's today's lesson?" I asked my inner voice.
"Trust. Yourself and others."

The entities I met out of my body were not always as friendly and benign as they were in the experience with the master and his students. I had an occasional run-in with astral entities who were not so friendly. I want to stress that negative experiences are extremely rare in the literature. The vast majority of OBEs seem to be positive and uplifting. Of the hundreds of OBEs I've had, only three were negative, and they're all presented in this chapter.

I had my first OBE encounter with negative entities in October of 1982. This morning I woke up early. I planned to go back to sleep, but I found myself in the best state of mind for an OBE. I knew exactly what I needed to do to get out of my body. I visualized that my midsection was swaying up and down. Then I sort of lifted myself above the scene. By an act of will, I moved into the midsection of the part that was swaying, and doing so, put my consciousness into my astral body.

Immediately, I came out of my body and was propelled forward. I looked around, but I didn't recognize my surroundings. I seemed to be in a completely astral atmosphere. The surrounding space was completely black, as if I were in deep space, but without stars.

Around me were objects and people. The people I saw didn't look evil, but they didn't look friendly either. One group of these people was to my right and about thirty feet away. There were about five men and women, and they were standing by an object that seemed to be a table of some sort. Their clothes looked awkward compared to today's fashions. They looked dirty. There were two men to my left, about twenty feet from each other. The one toward the rear was looking with anticipation, as if he were waiting for a little "fun." The nearest man looked like he was prepared to fight me. He looked mean and hostile and I had the distinct feeling that he intended to harm me. I could tell from the people's postures and facial expressions that I was being accosted by an astral lynch mob.

There was another man who was close to me, to my right, and I thought he was carrying a weapon, like a sword or a club. Obviously, he was holding the weapon in anticipation of using it on me. I thought, "Well, if I take off and fly right between them, I might be able to avoid harm." Then I thought, "But what if I get caught instead?" I looked at the man to my left. I thought, "I can probably defeat him without any trouble, but there are too many of them." Finally I just thought, "No way. I don't want any part of this. I'm not going to mess around. I'm not taking any chances. I'm getting out of here right now."

Not turning at all, I backed up and allowed myself to fall backward into my body. I blacked out for a second, then I woke up inside my body.

Since that experience, I've exercised a little more caution in my OBEs. How far can you trust a spirit? On the positive side, there are religions based on establishing contact with spirits,[5] which obviously involves a certain level of trust. Still, the Bible sternly warns people to not get involved with spirits,[6] so I've always had a general distrust of them.

Someone once asked me if I believed in ghosts. My basic response is, "Believe in ghosts? I *am* a ghost!" When I have an out-of-body experience, I'm in the same condition as a ghost. My point is this: When someone dies, they leave the body behind, and from that point on they're permanently a spirit. Dying doesn't necessarily make a person better (or more knowledgeable) than they were when they were alive. Just as there are living people with good and bad intentions, there are also dead people (spirits) with good and bad intentions. So I always approach spirits with a certain amount of caution, as illustrated by my second negative OBE which took place in March 1984.

This morning I was sick, so I had been dozing off and waking up for hours. I woke up, but I didn't realize I was out of my body. Suddenly, I heard a voice

---

[5]For example, the Spiritualist religion and the Spiritist religion founded by Allan Kardec.

[6]For example, the book of Leviticus has several warnings against fraternizing with spirits: "Do not resort to ghosts and spirits, not make yourselves unclean by seeking them out" (Leviticus 19:31). Also, see Leviticus 20:6, and 20:27.

coming from a specific point in the air above my feet. The voice surprised me a lot. I looked very hard, but I couldn't see any source for the voice. Still, I had heard spirit voices on rare occasions in the past, so it didn't bother me.

The voice was loud and clear. It was a man's voice, authoritative and commanding. It addressed me: "Robert Peterson, you must do exactly as I say. Speak the following words." The voice then said a word in a foreign language, and commanded me to repeat it.

I'm not stupid, and I don't trust spirits very much. The voice didn't seem malevolent, but I was leery of it anyway. I was sick, and I didn't feel strong enough to handle a potential danger. Deciding it was better to be polite, I mentally said directly to the voice, "I'm sorry, but there's no way. I don't even know you." I was still amazed that the voice was so loud and clear coming from nowhere.

Still, I wanted to say something, some words of power. I remembered some words that seemed power-ful from a song.[7] I spoke directly to the unknown voice and said the words from the song "Cocasaya Tay Toca." I don't know what the words mean, but it is a spiritual song, so I felt as if they were powerful words of spiritual love. The next thing I knew, I woke up inside my body. It was only then that I realized I had been out of my body.

Here is the third and final OBE (from October 1996) in which I felt unsafe or threatened:

I induced the OBE state, but my consciousness

---

[7]The song was "He Is Sailing" by the artists Jon and Vangelis, which appears on their 1983 album, *Private Collection*.

was not strong. I stood up and felt a pain in my left shoulder. Slightly bewildered, I turned around to see what could have caused the pain. To my surprise, there was an annoying-looking man there with a grin on his face.

I decided to try to get away from him, so I walked away, but he walked after me. He took another poke at my shoulder with his right hand, which sent another painful shock to my shoulder. I yelled at him, "Stop that!" Then I walked away again. I wasn't afraid at all. This time I tried to get away from him by quite a distance, but he followed me and kept zapping me. I yelled at him again, and used thought power to move to a location outside the house. Unfortunately, he followed me there, too, and zapped me again.

I decided that this pest would not leave me alone, so I deliberately ended the OBE.

The easiest way to avoid confrontations like this is to return to your body. Under most circumstances, simply thinking about your body will instantly bring you back to it.

Over time, I got rid of the fear and learned how to protect myself, both physically[8] and astrally. Several years later, I had an "almost-there experience,"[9] where I was surrounded by another angry mob, but this time

---

[8] I spent five years learning T'ai Chi Chuan and other forms of Chinese martial arts and movement exercises. T'ai Chi Chuan is a "soft style" (nonaggressive) Chinese martial art that is excellent for developing internal energy, self-defense, physical exercise, and meditation.

[9] See chapter 19 for an explanation of "almost-there experiences" and other consciousness-related phenomena.

I faced them fearlessly, fought them, and beat them up. Since that incident, I haven't been bothered anymore. I'll talk more about psychic protection for OBEs later in the book.

Most of my early exploring was done on my own. My general distrust of spirits usually kept me from interacting with them during my OBEs. Eventually, I learned that they can be very helpful in exploring the OBE world. You can go a lot farther with them than without them.

6

THE SOULMATE EXPERIENCE

While all around the pushing and prodding of
*   our feelings,*
The twisting and turning of our hearts,
Displaying an almost indefinable strength and
*   purpose, a reason, a reason, a reason*
Where no reasons seem to exist.
Yet as in a vision, a voice transcending all our
*   imagination*
Jewel of life, guiding light heralding a joyous new
*   dawn,*
Clear and gift of time, divine nature, super-nature
The supreme gift of knowledge and space, in this
*   cacophony of life*
Peace will come.

—Jon Anderson, Horizon

On August 19, 1982, I was with my brother and his wife on a camping trip, canoeing down the North Fork Crow River, just northwest of Minneapolis. We were on the last night of our trip, and had pushed ourselves hard to reach the small campsite before dark. Exhausted, we pitched our tents, ate our dinner, and went to bed. Everyone was too tired to say much, so we just went to bed.

After I climbed into my small one-person tent and snuggled into my sleeping bag, I fumbled around for my small flashlight. I clicked the flashlight on and pulled out my copy of Yogananda's book, *Autobiography of a Yogi*, and began reading where I'd left off the previous night.

I read for about an hour, as was my custom. Then I closed the book, shut off the flashlight, and set them both by my side and went to sleep.

Several hours later, at the edge of dawn, my body was still inanimate but I wasn't inside it. I became fully conscious and aware. In front of me was the most incredible woman I had ever seen, more attractive than the wildest fantasy I could have imagined. Notice I said "attractive," not "beautiful." She wasn't nearly as beautiful as some of my favorite television models, like Cheryl Ladd or Christie Brinkley, but she carried within her a magic, an attractiveness that I had never known in my twenty-one years. She had dark-brown hair that draped on her shoulders, and the most amazing eyes. I stared into her captivating eyes and reflected how to best describe her looks, if someone were to ask. Her features were attractive to me, but not stunningly beautiful as most men judge women. I carefully chose the words "beautiful to me" as my perfect description of her face.

Somehow, I knew this woman. We had been together many times before; in fact, I knew that she and I had chosen to come to this earthly existence together, as we had for many lifetimes. This wasn't just a friendship that bonded us together through our many lives; it was love. Until that morning, I had not known what true love was. My soul was burning inside with a passionate fire of love for her. This love consumed my every thought, my every motivation, my every desire. For the first time in my life, I felt like a complete person because I was with her. There was no longer a gaping hole of loneliness in my soul. She was mine and I was hers. I was with her and I had no intention of ever leaving. We were soulmates.

I was floating above her body, and I could see she was asleep, tossing and turning in obvious inner conflict and turmoil. Sleep is a place where we go to work on life's problems, and that's exactly what she was doing.

Because I was out of my body, I could communicate with her subconscious sleeping self. I could hear her thoughts and she could hear mine. She told me that a good friend of hers—a man—had asked her to marry him. She was tossing and turning because she couldn't decide whether she should marry him. She told me that he was a really good friend, the best friend she had ever had. He was kind and gentle and loving, and she knew that he loved her. She felt as if his proposal were the opportunity of a lifetime. She was lonely and she didn't want to throw away her only chance at having a loving husband and family. She was afraid of being alone and that it might be her last chance at love.

"Oh my God, nooooo!" I cried to her. "I love you. I want to marry you. Please don't do this to me. I need you. I beg you. I'll do anything, I promise." On and on I pleaded with her not to marry the man. My pleading only made her decision harder. "But what if this is my only chance? If I tell him no, he'll go away and I'll lose him as a friend. I'm afraid. I don't want to lose him. He'd make a good husband." Desperately I pleaded, "Listen to me: I *need* you. I *love* you. If you marry him, then what happens to us?" "But he loves me." "*I* love you. *I* will marry you. All I need is a chance. Please say no!" In a frenzy of emotion, I begged her, "Please, you've got to promise me you won't marry him."

Finally she said, "All right. I won't marry him." I could tell that her inner conflict was not yet over, however. She still had some thinking to do. Maybe she just said that to calm me. Nonetheless, I was relieved when I heard those words. My soul soared with joy and I gave a huge sigh of relief, saying, "Oh, thank God. You've just made me so happy. I love you."

I felt like I had just averted disaster. I looked deeply into her eyes and said, "I love you." I reached out my arms to embrace her, to hug her, to hold her for the rest of eternity, but something went terribly wrong.

As I reached out, I started getting farther and farther away, and I couldn't get close enough to touch her. I was being pulled back to my body. In horror, I watched her get farther and farther away from me. I screamed and clawed and fought and used everything within my power to get closer to her, all to no avail. Desperately, I looked at her and tried to memorize her face. Finally, she was out of sight.

I woke up in my tiny tent, alone.

Tears were streaming down my face. I cried. I'd never felt so alone, so betrayed. I repeated to myself, over and over, "She was real. I *know* she was real. I've got to find her." An abyss opened up in my soul. I was alone. I sobbed in my tent for more than an hour, until I heard my brother and his wife get up to start the day. I had just lost the only thing that was important to me (material things are not important to me because, as a spirit, I know some day we must leave them all behind).

Somehow I had to find the strength to get out of that tent. It was within that hour that I resolved to find her. I determined to let no other women into my life until I did. It was then that I turned my heart to steel.

For five solid days the memory of her face shone brightly in my mind; it haunted and teased me, like a photograph staring at me. Whenever I closed my eyes, I saw her face. For five days the image of her never left my closed eyelids.

Back home, I tried to sketch her, but it was beyond my ability. It would take a master to capture her hauntingly beautiful eyes. I decided that I couldn't do it justice, and that any half-drawn picture of her would only bias me later, so I tore the sketch up. After five days, her face was erased from my memory, but I believed I would recognize her if I ever saw her again.

"Where is my soulmate?" I asked my inner voice. It replied: "I can't tell you because that's part of your life-lesson." Sometimes the hardest lessons of our lives must be learned the hard way. If they were given to us easily, they wouldn't have the same value.

For many years I spent my life alone, searching for her, bearing my pain and longing for her. I let no other women enter my life; I was a closed door. You can't imagine the loneliness I felt. Every day I prayed to find her. Everywhere I went, I looked deeply into women's eyes, searching for "her," and every day I was disappointed. . . .

Before the soulmate experience, I had one quest: my spiritual development. I thought that I could live a spiritual life of contemplation alone. Spiritual seekers had been doing it for ages. Buddhist monks did it. Nuns and hermits did it. Ascetics did it. Saints did it. It seemed like the natural path for me to take. But the soulmate experience had affected me deeply. I had never believed in soulmates. I never realized how lonely I had been. Now I felt an emptiness inside that could only be filled by a lasting relationship.

From that point on my life had two purposes: to further my spiritual development, and to find the relationship I now desperately needed. But how could I find this soulmate of mine? Where would I look? She could be anywhere in the world.

7

THE JOANN LESSONS

"What's today's lesson?" I asked my inner voice.
"True love lets go."

Many months passed after the soulmate experience. I still hadn't found her, and the abyss in my soul got bigger, and my need for companionship grew stronger. I thought about using my OBE ability to try to locate her, but I decided I couldn't for several reasons.

First, there was a lot of emotional attachment there, so if I practiced with the intent of finding her, that emotional attachment would keep me firmly planted in my body. While inducing an OBE, you have to clear your mind of all thoughts and emotions, and that's impossible if you are thinking about your soulmate. Second, what if I actually found my soulmate during an OBE? That doesn't mean I could find her *physically.*[10] I was afraid that I'd have to endure another

---

[10] See chapter 21 for a discussion of problems locating people and things during an OBE.

painful experience of losing her again, and I couldn't take that chance. I couldn't bear to lose her again. I needed to find her physically, or not at all.

In the autumn of 1983, I returned home to start my senior year at the university. One day early in the quarter, I went for a walk by the Mississippi River where there was a small patch of woods. I stretched my psychic awareness as wide open as possible, and soon I was flooded with joy on a wonderful fall day. With my mind, I could feel the "souls" of the trees surrounding me as I walked through the woods. When no one was looking, I did something I had never done before: I hugged a tree, letting my joy mingle with the soul of the tree. For a few minutes, I wept tears of joy.

Walking away from the tree, I said to my inner voice, "Okay, I'm ready for my next lesson." My inner voice replied, "There are two paths you can take, and you must choose which path. The first path is an easy path, but it affords less spiritual growth. The second path is a very difficult path, but it will maximize your spiritual growth." I thought about it for a long time, then I asked, "Will I be able to handle the difficult path?" My inner voice reminded me that we are never given a problem without also having the ability to solve it. My mind was still soaring with joy. "I choose the difficult path," I said. My inner voice asked, "Are you sure?" I said, "Yes." And it replied, "So be it."

The "difficult path" began the second week of class, on a Monday morning, some time after eleven o'clock. I was sitting in a computer class called "Introduction to Higher Level Languages." Boredom overtook me because I had a natural knack for computers and knew the subject matter very well. I preferred to focus on more spiritual pursuits.

My psychic abilities were in full swing, and I used them as a form of entertainment. On this occasion, I decided to do some mind traveling. This is not out-of-body travel, but is more akin to remote viewing, which is easier than out-of-body travel.[11] I picked a person at random, an Asian man, and reached out to him with my mind. I took note of how different his thoughts were from those of most Westerners. Still, this man was very much concerned with physical things. His life was centered on modern technology. I decided it was time to move on, so I sent my mind to another man. He was thinking lazily about his girlfriend, and wishing very badly that he could be with her. I stayed there a little while, then left.

At random, I picked out another person, a woman this time. I reached out and touched her mind. Touching her mind was like touching a live electrical power line. I was suddenly overcome by a mass of emotions. There were high vibrations inside her that hit me, carrying me deep to the center of her soul. My own vibrations were pulled higher until I thought my own soul would shatter under the pressure.

When I reached the center, I heard three words, simple in meaning and yet explosive in their ramifications: "We are one." The sound of these words echoed back and forth across my mind for minutes that seemed like hours. I was floored by what I had experienced, so I withdrew my mind, back across the room into my own head. What could possibly be within her to cause such a tremendous feeling within me? I

---

[11]For more information on remote viewing, see *Mind Trek: Exploring Consciousness, Time, and Space Through Remote Viewing* by Joseph McMoneagle.

studied her face. To the eye, she looked like a normal woman, certainly not any more attractive than average.

Perhaps my mind traveling had gone astray. I decided to try it again just to be sure. Once again, I closed my eyes and reached my mind out to touch her soul, and once again I was struck by these explosive vibrations, these pure, high thoughts of heaven, and this sea of love. Once again, when I reached the center, the words "We are one" echoed across my soul. I had reached a portion of heaven and I had no desire to leave. Leave? The thought never crossed my mind. Eventually the class was over, and with much difficulty, I yanked myself from the music of her soul. The rest of the day a warm glow stayed with me and I continually heard the echoes of "We are one."

The next time I saw her, I repeated the experiment, and the feelings only became stronger and stronger. I was a computer programmer; I understood logic and analysis, not emotions. I was confused by my feelings and tried to sort them out, but my feelings defied logic. I tried to explain to my brother Joe that I had feelings for this woman, and he said, "What does your inner voice tell you?" Of course! I had been too entranced by the experience to stop and ask my inner voice. Later that day, I asked my inner voice, "What is happening to me?" The reply was simple, direct, and unmistakable: "Duh, stupid! You've fallen in love with her." I was shocked. I had had girlfriends but never before had I "fallen in love." Since my soulmate experience, I hadn't taken any relationship seriously.

"So this is love," I thought to myself. "We are one." There was nothing at all sexual about it; my feelings were purely spiritual.

I wanted to go out with her, but every time I saw her, she was with someone, and it seemed like there was no way to talk to her. I prayed to my guides, asking them for a chance to talk with her alone. Such requests are never ignored, so a few days later it was granted. I ran into her "by accident" in the hallway at school. I asked if sometime I could buy her lunch so we could talk. She seemed happy about this and said that it would be possible. Her name was JoAnn. While talking to her, I felt as if I were being bombarded with intense, high-pitched vibrations. My mind wanted to let go and fly aimlessly. I don't remember exactly what I said, but I ended up making a fool of myself.

Both she and I were too busy to meet even for lunch due to the unusually harsh obligations of another class, "Software Engineering." That particular class was the hell of my life. The pressure was so intense that I was working myself to the point of exhaustion every night, which went on for two quarters. Those two quarters at the university were so bad that any minor escape was a relief. I enjoyed going to work (a relatively tough computer programming job) just to get away from the pressure of school. Between school, work, and sleep, I had no free time. I had no life outside of those three functions, and I had a lot of trouble coping. I was edgy and irritable. My feelings and mind grew numb from the stress. In retrospect, it seems amazing to me that I didn't have a nervous breakdown.

Time passed and my infatuation grew. Due to my work load at school, all I could do was continue to work on my school and work projects. Desperately, I tried to talk to her again. Once again, I made a fool of myself, and came away loving her and hating myself.

As more time passed, I was "coincidentally" given personal information about her. I learned her address, phone number, and roommate's name, all completely "by accident." I even consulted the tarot, which was positive regarding her. But why, I wondered, was I continually kept away from her?

I needed some kind of release to break through all the numbness, exhaustion, and frustration I kept pent up inside. I found that release in the form of heavy-metal music. A friend of mine listened to heavy metal, and he lent me a few albums. Much to my amazement, it was the perfect outlet. Years later, I still listen to some heavy metal, but as strange as it may seem, I feel a warm glow of love and spirituality as I listen, not any negativity. Heavy-metal music is just another form of entertainment, like a good Stephen King horror novel.

As time passed, I neared the time of my graduation, and I realized that I might never see JoAnn again. Finally, I talked to her through a computer chat program. She made it clear that she wasn't interested in me. I lost her.

I knew I had to let go of JoAnn. I withdrew my selfishness and replaced it with pure love. My inner voice said, "True love lets go." So I wished her to follow her own path, and I resolved to follow mine.

To console myself, I told myself that JoAnn was just a distraction from the soulmate I had seen the year before. Once again, I set a firm resolution to find that soulmate.

Many years have passed, and it's all water under the bridge. Through this experience, I learned that

• True love is not selfish. I had two loves for JoAnn: selfish and unselfish. My selfish love wanted JoAnn to be mine forever. My unselfish love knew that it was more important for her to be happy and free than with me.

• True love lets go. I was clinging too tightly. Parents must face this painful realization when they must let their children go out into the world, even if they will be hurt.

• True love cannot be halted by rejection.

• True love causes no pain and knows no pain.

• You can love someone without knowing them.

• True love needs nothing in return.

My experience with JoAnn helped me to develop my theory of the relativity of love: Stated simply, it says that everything Einstein said about light also applies to love.

Einstein's theory of relativity states that matter and energy are relative, and light is a constant. If one car travels in one direction at ten miles per hour, and another car travels in the opposite direction at ten miles per hour, then each car is traveling at twenty miles per hour, relative to the other. However, if each of those cars carries a light, the light waves have the same speed in all directions, and not twenty miles per hour faster or slower in any direction. In terms of love, I believe that when we love anyone or anything, our love spreads throughout all that is in all directions; we are, in effect, loving all that is, but using another person as our focal point.

One frequency of electromagnetic radiation does not interfere with other frequencies (for instance, many radio stations can occupy the same space and time). In the same way, I believe that one love will never interfere with another love. This means, for instance, that the love we have for our friends and family will not diminish our love for our spouses or lovers. This also means that you don't need to stop feeling love for one person in order to start loving another. Love always accepts other love. This leaves no room for jealousy. Love is *not* possessive.

Light is eternal, not bounded. An unobstructed light that is shining will continue to travel through outer space forever, without becoming "less." It may seem to diminish because it spreads and expands to cover more area. Love is also unbounded. Once we feel love, that love continues to exist in some form, even if we don't feel it anymore. This also means that love is never wasted. For instance, even if we suffer a bitter breakup and now hate our former partner's guts, we can still look back on the happier times without regretting that they ever happened.

Love never limits us. It is unlimited. When light hits an object, it is either reflected or absorbed, increasing the object's energy, or both. By the same token, when we feel love for someone, it either "warms" that person or is passed on, or both.

Light, when focused and directed (like telescopes and microscopes) permits us to see things that are out of the reach of our senses. Love, when it is focused and directed, also permits us to see things. It permits us to learn about people and things, which would be unknowable without that love. What is more important, it permits us to learn about ourselves. Love expands our horizons. Perhaps love is the source of all psychic awareness.

I believe that love holds no fear. Fear is a result of making assumptions and expectations, and I believe that love makes no assumptions, and holds no expectations about anyone or anything. Love never takes anything or anyone for granted.

Love is unconditional acceptance. Love means that the innermost you is okay. Love prefers the real you, and not someone who is pretending or wearing masks. And by the same rule, love accepts everyone else as they are.

Love doesn't apply to images, ideals, or our ideas of a person, not even our images of ourselves. Love applies only to the real person above and beyond the images. The joy in love is not in the receiving, but the giving. Just as Einstein said that matter and energy are one, so too I believe that love comprises all that is, binding the very atoms together. For in a world where everything is relative, love itself is the only absolute.

8

PEGGY'S GIFT

*"What's today's lesson?" I asked my inner voice.
"Today, live without expectations."*

I managed to make it through my senior year at the university with my sanity intact, but barely. My dabbling with mind travel had gotten me obsessed with JoAnn, and now that I had lost her, I was leery of doing any more psychic dabbling. I had almost had a nervous breakdown and was in bad shape. I was still without my soulmate, and now that I had graduated, I felt lost and without direction.

I spent a few more years in Minneapolis looking for the woman from my soulmate experience. I searched the Minneapolis area for her, and came up empty. In July of 1985, I decided to get a fresh start, so I moved to Phoenix to spend some time in the sun, healing.

My first order of business was to join two metaphysical discussion groups, hoping to find my soulmate there. The first group studied the books of Seth, an entity channeled by author Jane Roberts. The second group conversed with a channeled entity called Nect. It was great to finally be able to talk with like-minded people who had experiences similar to mine. I didn't find my soulmate in either of the groups, but I developed close friendships with some wonderful people.

One of my best friends from the discussion groups was Peggy, a petite, powerful woman who was beautiful, talented, intelligent, and very independent. She had a slender build and delicate fingers that were capable of masterfully playing the piano, working on cars, or doing any other task that she set out to do. I always thought of Peggy as my sister; in fact, she was a lot like my real sister, Cathy.

Peggy gave me a gift in the form of an unconscious lesson. That is to say, she did not give me this lesson consciously. Perhaps it was not Peggy who gave the lesson, but rather an angel, a spirit guide, or maybe my higher self. The lesson is one of the most important ones of my life.

Nearly four years had passed since my soulmate experience. The lesson began with an ordinary dream on July 11, 1986. I dreamed I was at one of the discussion groups, and that we were planning a trip. I was planning to travel alone on this trip. Then something unusual happened. Usually my dreams seem to follow some kind of unconscious script. Somehow the dream had thrown out the script and was no longer following its planned path, and the dream took an unexpected twist.

In the dream, just as we were about to set out on the trip, Peggy walked up to me. She looked deeply into my eyes for a moment, then, still looking into my eyes, she said, "I love you." I knew that she meant it in a romantic way. I responded, "I love you, too." She knew I meant it and we embraced. Somehow our minds merged and became one, so that our thoughts, feelings, and emotions were the same. It was not sexual. Our souls simply joined and became one. I had her skill on the piano, and her knowledge of music; she had my knowledge of computers. There were no longer two bodies embracing; there was a single body, the focus of our single consciousness. We were happily one soul.

I woke up from the dream bewildered. I had never been interested in Peggy as a lover. In my mind, she was my sister. Confused, I struggled to figure out why I had this dream and what it meant. In the end, I wrote it off as nonsense from my subconscious, and forgot it.

The next night, I had another dream about Peggy, a dream in which we agreed to share a car ride together. The car went out of control, but we managed to avoid an accident. I awoke, still confused about why I was dreaming about Peggy.

The "Peggy dreams" continued, and each night they got a little bit more involved. At night, we were talking, playing music for each other, and growing closer. At the time, it seemed as if I were on the verge of a romantic dream-relationship with the dream-Peggy, even though we were just friends in real life. This was baffling, since I had no romantic intentions for Peggy.

I was confused about the dreams and why I was having them. The best solution to problems like this is to examine your beliefs, and that's what I did. I picked apart my beliefs concerning relationships. The first thing I discovered was that several times I had become enamored or infatuated with someone's image (what I saw or perceived), rather than the real person (their soul). I, of all people, should realize that a person's physical body is only a vehicle and is not what's important. Soul transcends race, color, sexual orientation. If everyone would learn to see people as "soul" or "spirit" instead of "body," perhaps there would be no more prejudice or hate crimes.

Sometimes we can be held back by our own limiting beliefs. My inner voice drove this home by guiding me through the following exercise. It said, "Think about your friend Cindy. What do you like most about her?" I thought to myself: "I like her because she makes me feel comfortable; I can talk with her and share my feelings with her, and she can share hers with me, and neither of us feels threatened. We're not competing, not engaging each other, not demanding anything, not expecting anything; we're just sharing a mutual experience. We are rejoicing in each other's existence. When I'm with Cindy, I don't have to be anything or anyone: no images to uphold, no reputation to protect, no ego to support. I am perfectly comfortable and content with myself, and I accept her as she is."

My inner voice said, "Now think about your soulmate, as you normally imagine her." When I did that I suddenly felt uncomfortable. I realized something was wrong with my beliefs, so I followed the feeling back to its source. I discovered I had unwittingly placed my soulmate on a pedestal. She was no longer a person; she was an ideal, a goal, an object, a fantasy. Somehow I hadn't left any room for humanity in my beliefs about her. When I realized that, there was a release. I had let go of a very limiting belief. I stopped worshiping my soulmate and started loving her.

Even after these realizations, my lesson was not over. The Peggy dreams continued. In another dream, Peggy and I were still "just friends," but we lived together in a castle, and were entertaining guests. In another dream, I was working on a computer program when, to my astonishment, the computer started printing messages about Peggy on the screen.

In yet another dream, Peggy asked me if she could walk with me. In another, Peggy asked if she could move in with me. Then I dreamed that Peggy made sexual advances to me. I was shocked. The Peggy dreams culminated with this last dream. It was set in the future, several years after the time frame of the others:

I was back in Minnesota. The morning had been cold. I had spent the better part of it helping people get their cars unstuck after a heavy Minnesota snowfall. I was with a group of people, all bustling about the city streets, helping one another. It had started to warm up and the snow was melting, so I went inside to join a party.

Once inside, I noticed there was no music. "Not much like a party," I thought, so I went over to the small portable cassette player on the floor. I picked up a nearby tape and looked at it. It had no label and was not rewound. I popped the tape in and pressed the play button. Piano music came over the speakers, followed by the magical voice of Brad Delp:

> And, feelin' the way I do
> Wouldn't last a mile without you.
> When I'm losin' the way
> The things that you say
> Take me there—my destination
> My destination
> Is by your side
> Right by your side (Scholtz 1986)

This was a party tape I had recorded long ago. There were some light rock songs and some hard rock songs. Peggy didn't like the hard rock music, so I switched the tape off and pulled it out. Peggy came over to my side. "Who is that? I like that," she asked sweetly. "It's Boston, from their *Third Stage* album," I replied. She wanted me to stop fooling around with the tapes and join the party. "Why don't you just play that for a while," she said. "Okay," I said, "Let me rewind it first." I rewound the tape and once again pressed play. Heavy-metal guitarist Yngwie Malmsteen started playing. I cringed. Peggy hated Malmsteen. Still, this song was pretty tame, so I turned it down and joined the party.

Bob W. and Sabrina were in our living room, plus two other couples. All the chairs were occupied in the small living room of our small house, so I sat on the floor. There was a moment of intense silence in which everyone felt uncomfortable. Bob W. broke the silence. "So, Bob," he asked, "How do you like living with a pianist?" As friendly as he intended to be, his question made me feel very uncomfortable. I was never at ease talking about my relationships with others. That was a little too personal for my comfort.

Peggy and I had decided to move into this house and had been living together for about a month. Getting along with Peggy wasn't always easy, but it had its moments. We were happy. It was a decision we had made, and we were glad we made it. We had our spats and disagreements, but we loved each other, so we worked things out. The good outweighed the bad tenfold. Still, to say we always got along wouldn't be accurate.

It was none of their business, I thought to myself, how well Peggy and I got along. I was in love with

Peggy, and I was glad we were living together. This was a party, and it shouldn't be spoiled with heavy talk about relationships. I wanted something cute and funny to say, to satisfy Bob and change the subject at the same time.

How do I like living with a pianist? At last I spoke with a short laugh. "Me? Huh, I can't tell one note from another." I glanced over to Peggy to see her reaction to my statement. A tear formed in her eye and her lip trembled. She stood up sobbing and grabbed her purse. "I'm sorry." Her voice was broken. "Go on without me. I have to go."

Oh no! She must have misunderstood me. "Act quickly," I thought. "I can't stand to see her leave." I didn't want to hurt her. "Peggy! Wait! I can explain! Please!" Even if she had listened, she would have been too embarrassed by her outburst. "Excuse me," I said to our guests, and walked outside.

"Peggy, let me explain what I meant." She just stood there sobbing. I felt terrible. "I wasn't trying to say that your playing was bad, I only meant to say how bad and untrained my ear is. You know I love your music. Your playing is beautiful. I just felt uncomfortable about Bob's question, and I needed to change the subject."

She looked up at me. There were still tears welling in her eyes, but we looked in each other's eyes and it was a look of understanding. Her eyes turned down. Her voice was still a little weak. "God damn it, anyway," she said with despair in her voice, "Just when you think you've got your life together, some guy comes along and you fall in love, and everything gets all screwed up. I can't think straight anymore. I don't know what to feel anymore. I don't even know what I want anymore."

Peggy looked up once more and quickly kissed me on the lips. We fell into each other's arms and hugged. Neither of us knew where our lives were going, but we knew we were in love, and that was enough. I immediately woke up, shocked by the dream.

In a desperate attempt to understand the baffling dreams, I probed deeper into my beliefs concerning relationships. I discovered that my relationship problems all boiled down to one thing: expectations. It was part of the same "image" thing. I was expecting Peggy and everyone else on Earth to act in certain ways and do certain things. When people didn't meet my expectations, I was disappointed, or I manufactured a "problem" in my mind. We all do it. Most of the time it happens so quickly and so far below the surface that we don't even notice.

Now that I had seen through the problem, it was like a veil was lifted and I could see clearly. As my spiritual sister, I had expected Peggy to act like my sister. The dreams had broken through that veil and blown away my expectations of her.

My expectations had been my limiting factor. I sometimes get frustrated in traffic because I expect drivers to follow certain conventions, and when they don't I get frustrated because they don't do *what I want* them to do. They were just being themselves, and that wasn't good enough for me!

My inner voice stepped in with the following: "Congratulations. This is Peggy's gift to you. Although she may not realize it consciously, she agreed to participate and cast those images in your dreams. She agreed to say, 'I love you' in that dream, to allow this all to happen, to bring you to this realization. Although she may not realize it consciously, she broke your expectations to enable you to learn this lesson. You were dealing with an ideal, an expectation, an image, a phantom, a fantasy, instead of a person. The same goes for JoAnn and others. There are no 'shoulds' with people."

Suddenly I was released from all expectations. It was like a tremendous burden had been lifted from my shoulders. My love shouted out to the universe in joyous splendor. I no longer needed anything from anyone. I was self-sufficient. I didn't need my soulmate. I desired her, yes, but I didn't need her. I cast away my images. What Peggy lies above and beyond my image? How wonderful she is, without my expectations. She is herself, perfectly, wonderfully. Everyone is! I am no longer "stuck" inside the box of my own expectations. Now there is a new reality, one where everyone is unique and exciting. The "unexpected" action of another person is an overlapping of realities, where the edges of two realities touch in an unexplainable intimacy. All life is sharing this kind of intimacy. This knowledge is Peggy's gift.

I feel alive and free inside, like I never have before. Nothing is so serious anymore. Having no expectations, I can give my love away joyously, freely, happily. I have no expectations for anyone to live up to. Now I feel free to do anything or say anything I want. How do I expect people to react? I don't. I want it to be a surprise. That way, nothing they could possibly do can fall short of my expectations. If they place their expectations on me, that's their problem, not mine.

With the realization of Peggy's gift, the Peggy dreams stopped, and my confusion was over. The dreams all had a special purpose. I believe that Peggy, my spiritual sister, was subconsciously influencing, directing, and acting out situations in my dreams for one purpose, to teach me this lesson: Expect nothing. Life will become a wonderment of surprise, and you will never be disappointed or let down.

9

ON SOULMATES

*Spirituality has a common base, and it is all
    connected
by one fundamental principle. Any guesses?*
                                    —Inner Voice

In mid-September, 1986, after the lesson of Peggy's gift, I once again resumed my quest to find my soulmate. This time I decided to consult my inner voice. For several nights, I asked my inner voice about my soulmate, and typed the answers into my computer. Here are some excerpts:

What's today's lesson?
    Today's lesson is about expectations. Through Peggy's gift, you know that your expectations were interfering with your ideal relationship. What were some of your expectations?

I expected my soulmate to be about my age, and to have shoulder-length, dark hair. I expected that she would like the same things I do, like metaphysics. Suppose she's a fundamentalist Christian?
    Your friend Cindy was once a fundamentalist "born again" Christian. It's not a terminal illness; it can be cured!

Cindy is understanding. Even though she was a born-again Christian, I could talk to her about the things I believe are spiritual if I used her language.

If your soulmate were a fundamentalist, what would that mean?

It would probably mean that she thinks everything that I believe to be spiritual really comes from the Devil. It would mean that she is dogmatic and it would be almost impossible to knock any spiritual sense into her head.

Even if that were so, could you still live with her?

How can two people live together, believing that the other lives a misguided, unspiritual life?

Yet each is very spiritual in their own way. Remember this. Spirituality has a common base, and it is all connected by one fundamental principle. Any guesses?

Love?

You win the booby prize! In more sense "booby" than you realize. You can and should live and cooperate together in love regardless of your differences because your love keeps you together. It pushes you toward a common goal, and helps you to smooth out your differences. Each of you has your idiosyncrasies and dogmas, but each of you is an accomplished arbitrator. Eventually you both will grow closer together in harmony.

But what if I eventually accept her beliefs and become a born-again Christian? I don't want that. That's the opposite of spirituality.

No, the opposite of spirituality is apathy. If you decide to accept Christianity, it will be on your own terms, and you would be comfortable with that change. It would not be anything against your will. There you go again—worrying about losing control. This time you worry about losing control of your own beliefs.

That's because I'm very wary of my own beliefs; I saw how I had followed blind paths when I left the Catholic Church.

And yet that was a very valuable steppingstone. You took on those beliefs from your mother, and those beliefs served you well, until your inner self reached for more. You knew with your inner being that spirituality is more than sitting and praying in a church. It is living. It is ongoing. You cannot accept beliefs against your will. There is no such thing as doing anything "against your will," because you have complete control over your reality, and the key to it all is the will.

Your soulmate is not a fundamentalist Christian. She may or may not be into metaphysics as you know it; I will not say. But this exercise is meant to help you take down a few more of your limitations. Suppose she has purple Mohawk hair? Suppose she is overweight? Suppose she is much older or younger? You must be willing to accept her regardless. Love knows no boundaries. As long as you keep placing boundaries, love will have a very difficult time in projecting itself outward and inward. Say this: "Soulmate, I accept you in my heart."

Soulmate, I accept you in my heart.

For now and forever.

For now and forever.

I place no limitations on you: body, soul, life, circumstances, knowledge, intelligence or spirituality.

Even spirituality?

Even spirituality. What if she chooses to learn spirituality in this life, and has little of it now?

Okay. I place no limitations on you: body, soul, life, circumstances, knowledge, intelligence or spirituality.

And in all respects.

And in all respects.

Marriage vows should not become a series of limitations, such as "I will not make love with another. I will not fight or argue." Your love will ensure those things. Instead, marriage vows should be a set of freedoms: "I give you the freedom to be yourself, I give you the freedom to express yourself to me in any and all ways. I give you the freedom to forever vent your love in my direction. I give you the freedom to express your sexuality with me. I give you the freedom to laugh and play and act silly without fear of my ridicule or attack in any form. I give you the freedom to express and enact your love for me and for others, in whatever way you most desire, whether I am focused in physical life, or not."

I finally finished reading The Harmony of Love *(Larzelere 1982). I wrote down a couple of issues from the book and I want you to comment on them. It said that soulmates are not found, but are created out of total responsibility, freedom, love, and hard work. I'm not sure I like that.*

It depends upon your definition of soulmates. By the author's definition, and by what he believes, that is entirely true. Most people have a very limited and restrictive definition of soulmates. A soulmate is not two halves of a soul, nor is it two people who are "forever bound to keep returning to physical life together."

The term "soulmates" refers to two people who have a very strong attraction and love, and they decide to incarnate physically and plan to enter into a loving relationship with each other. Although they may share more than one lifetime together, that is decided before each lifetime, and also what type of relationship they plan to share. Of course, their plans may change during that lifetime. It does not exclude the possibility of two such relationships. For instance, Jane Roberts and Rob Butts decided long before they were born to discover each other in "new personality essence" forms. They shared a wonderful and cooperative life together, learning much and teaching much. That in no way limits Rob to that one relationship now that Jane has passed on. Not everybody comes into this lifetime with such an agreement, so not everyone has a soulmate.

Since each personality learns, grows, and develops in their lives, each person has a unique learning, ego, and experience base; therefore, their oversouls are very much in love and know each other quite well, from ages past. But, the individual personalities do not know each other, and therefore must rediscover each other. In this way, they must create a new relationship for themselves, and that's where the total responsibility and hard work come into play. It is true that a soulmate relationship is an agreement, like any shared event, but it is also true that a soulmate relationship, like all relationships, must truly be created in the most basic sense of that word. And in that sense, what the book says is quite valid.

The fact is, at this moment, you do not know your soulmate in this lifetime. That rapport and relationship must be created and built upon. You once experienced being with your soulmate, and you once again affirmed your love for each other. Your knowledge stemmed from the knowledge of your greater self, your oversoul. In that sense, you are very familiar with each other, but insofar as your ego is concerned, beyond that experience, you have never met. You have chosen this lifetime to begin anew, to re-create that soulmate relationship.

The book said that soulmates are not found. Well, there is some truth to this statement. Having a soulmate relationship is more than just the finding of that person. Once she is found, then what do you do? Most people hope and pray to find their soulmate, but there is so much more than the finding. Suppose they find them, then what? The meeting or finding is just the beginning, and really a very trivial part of the relationship.

Aren't you glad you didn't find your soulmate years ago? If you found each other when you were a Catholic, your relationship would be a very difficult one indeed.

On the other hand, if she found you any earlier, your personality would not be as complete, experienced, or spiritual as it is now. You have both chosen to be apart so that you may once again be pulled together with a greater knowledge and experience, and this will result in a greater love and learning for each of you. To this end, it is truly a blessing that you are not together at this moment, even though it may seem like a curse.

Do not concentrate on the negative. Do not grieve over her absence, your loss, for this only serves to strengthen that absence, and your feelings in that direction. Instead, concentrate upon the positive. Think to yourself, "It has been good for both of us to be apart, but there is no more need to be apart. I suggest that we find each other and meet, and begin to share the love and growth we both want." As you say this, your soulmate will pick up on it and your meeting will be made firmer in this reality and closer to this time period. Do this with all sincerity and love in your heart, not with grief or negativism.

59

And as you sow, so shall you reap!

I have one more note from the book The Harmony of Love. *It is a quotation I liked. It said that love is allowing the relationship to unfold. It is not forcing issues, demanding decisions. It is not making the relationship happen.*

The most important part of that statement is "not making the relationship happen." It's also been said, "Don't push the river." Rivers are wonderful things, don't you think? We've talked about rivers before; I could talk about them for endless hours. Relationships are like rivers, and as such they should be allowed to flow naturally. They will find their own guidance. They will have their sand bars, and white water, but they always find their destination, without looking, without rushing. The relationship, like a river, will happen by itself. This means you should not make unnecessary expectations and demands upon it. You should not be continually looking for what you are "getting out" of the relationship, for the relationship should be its own reward. In other words, don't go fishing in the river; just joyfully play in its waters.

10

CATHY

All prayers are answered, and they're answered for our highest good. Unfortunately, they're not always answered the way we'd like them to be.

—Inner Voice

In late 1986, I was still living in Phoenix. I was doing some freelance computer consulting at the time, but I barely made enough money to survive.

One day a woman came to one of the discussion groups. Her face seemed familiar, almost as if we had met before, but at first glance, she didn't spark any memories from my soulmate experience. Still, there were some coincidences. Her eyes were big and had a beautiful dark-brown color. I remembered that my soulmate had special, dark-brown eyes. Just like my soulmate, the woman also had shoulder-length dark-brown hair. "Okay," I thought to myself, "calm down. She's got two of the same features, but the recognition isn't there. What other features can I look at?" She wasn't stunningly beautiful, but she had all the physical features I liked in a woman; in fact, the best way to describe her was "beautiful to me," and I had also used those words to describe the woman from the soulmate experience.

When she introduced herself to the group as Cathy, my mind was reeling. The name Cathy (or Kathy) is a special name in my family. My sister's name is Cathy. My oldest brother, Don, married a woman named Kathy. My second-oldest brother, Tom, also married a woman named Kathy. I didn't discriminate against women with other names, but somehow in my heart, I felt it was my destiny to also marry a woman named Kathy or Cathy.

After the group meeting, Cathy was talking with someone across the room. Although I couldn't hear what they said, they pointed at me as if to say, "Talk to that guy over there." Cathy walked over to me, but instead of introducing herself, she simply said, "I've seen you before. In a dream." My mind was racing. Most astral travelers believe that dreams are unconscious out-of-body experiences. Was she the one? This was too intense. "Really? You saw me in a dream?" I tried to pry some more information out of her, but she wouldn't go into details. Someone had told her that I could leave my body, and she wanted to talk about that instead. Still, I couldn't help but wonder if she was hiding her experience from me because it was too personal.

"Is Cathy the one?" I asked my inner voice. Once again, I got the same reply: "I can't tell you because it's part of your life-lesson."

As we became friends, I learned more about Cathy. She was married, and although she didn't remember the exact date, her engagement probably happened near the time of my soulmate experience. I still didn't recognize her as the woman from the soulmate experience, however. Her eyes, although beautiful, were not the same eyes I had seen in 1982. After careful consideration, I decided not to get involved with her. Cathy and I remained "just friends."

As the mild winter of Phoenix approached in late 1986, one day I asked my inner voice, "When will I meet my soulmate?" All it said was "Soon." Later, I went to a friend's house and we started playing with a Ouija board. I asked the Ouija the same question, "When will I meet my soulmate?" and I got a much more direct answer. It said I would meet her "Next October."

In the holiday season of 1986, I visited my family in Minnesota. I finally decided to see if an OBE could help me in my search for my soulmate. I had one on January 1, 1987.

Drifting off to sleep at my mom's apartment in Minneapolis, I found myself in a good near-OBE state. With little effort, I started mind-swaying. I used the momentum to stand up out of my body. I was a bit disoriented and had trouble with my balance.

I was sharing the double bed with my brother Joe during the stay in Minneapolis. Since he was moving around, I figured he was conscious, so I decided to try to make my body talk. I tried a bunch of things, but no sound was produced that my astral ears could hear, and Joe later said he heard nothing.

I decided to try meditating during the OBE to see what it was like. I took a few steps away from the bed, turned around, lifted both hands at the elbow, in a praying posture. I closed my eyes and thought very strongly, "I wish peace and love to the universe." Then I reached my mind out to the universe with love, similar to one of my favorite meditations.

I unexpectedly felt the touch of a hand on my right shoulder. That startled me and I opened my astral eyes to see what spirit, angel, or entity touched me. I couldn't see anyone nearby, so I reasoned that the entity must have vibrations much higher and more spiritual than mine, and that's why I couldn't see him or her.

I spent a few seconds trying to contact the entity with my mind, with no results. I wondered for a few seconds whether or not I should be afraid because I was obviously affected by an astral person I could not see. Could it harm me? Could it take over my body? Finally I decided not to worry about it.

I decided to just have as much fun as I possibly could on this OBE. I started wildly, weightlessly dancing, jumping, and flailing my arms up to the sky, playing like a little kid. I ran in all directions, through the walls of my mom's apartment. I jumped up, sometimes landing three or four feet in midair. Sometimes I landed on the floor like a crunched-up accordion. Other times I landed halfway through the floor into the apartment below.

After a few minutes of this silliness, I got more serious and practical. I decided to visit someone and wondered whom to pick as my target. I decided I'd try to visit my soulmate. I closed my eyes and jumped up with the idea of my soulmate in my mind, but I blacked out and went into a very strange dream.

The experiment was unsuccessful. Some OBE authors have said that too much emotion can end an out-of-body experience. I wondered if an OBE would ever help me find my soulmate, or if I had too much emotion invested there. I knew I'd try again someday.

11

THE EDGE OF THORNS

A study made from winter,
Of summers long ago,
And dreams that used to glitter,
Safely now hidden under snow.
                                        —Savatage, "Edge of Thorns"

Before returning to Phoenix in early 1987, my brother talked me into interviewing for a computer job in Rochester, Minnesota. The company that interviewed me was desperate for good computer programmers, so they made me an offer I couldn't refuse. It seemed like the universe was giving me a hint: I had searched Arizona for two disappointing years. Maybe my soulmate was in Minnesota after all. I returned to Phoenix only long enough to close my bank accounts, pack my belongings into a moving truck, and leave. I drove through a blizzard, but arrived safely in Rochester.

After a few weeks of intense training, I was finally ready to start my job as a contract programmer at the largest computer plant in the world. My new boss took me from office to office to introduce me to the programmers I'd be working with. After meeting four of my new mentors, I was led into the office of a fifth.

When my eyes met the woman inside the office, I was stunned. She had the same hauntingly beautiful eyes of the woman from my soulmate experience. "Oh my God," I thought to myself, "I think I found her." She had all the physical characteristics I described in the soulmate experience: the same shoulder-length dark-brown hair, the same build. She was not a knock-out, but "beautiful to me." There was an intense sense of recognition, yet somehow I still wasn't convinced. I thought I would remember more from the soulmate experience. It can't be this easy. Was she my soulmate? It had been five years since the soulmate experience, so I didn't know if I could be sure based on a faded memory. Maybe she was, maybe she wasn't. Either way, I recognized her, and it wasn't from this lifetime. I felt uncontrollably attracted to her and it was an attraction that went beyond space and time.

There was a problem, however. I was a contractor, and she was technically my client, so I couldn't fraternize with her at all. I had to remain calm and keep everything on a professional level. Somehow I managed to keep my composure, but my mind was on her, not on my job, so I ended up looking and acting like a fool.

"Is she the one?" I asked my inner voice. I got the same reply, "I can't tell you because it's part of your life-lesson." Damn it!

That night when I closed my eyes, in front of my closed eyelids I saw her face, just as I had with my soulmate experience. The feeling was unusual and intense because I don't have a photographic memory; except for my soulmate experience, this had never happened to me before and it's never happened since. As much as I wanted to, I couldn't force myself to see anything but her face when I closed my eyes that night. The details of her face were so clear that I drew a small sketch of her, hoping that putting her on paper would help get her out of my mind.

The next day at work, I gave her the sketch. I had the same feeling of recognition when I saw her, but this time I was a little more observant: I noticed that she was wearing a wedding ring.

At first I felt angry. Act like nothing's wrong. Then I felt betrayed. I must not show my feelings. I felt betrayed, not only by her but by God, who I felt had kept me alive with the promise of a soulmate, and who had now taken that hope away. My soulmate had promised not to get married. Was this the same woman? If this were the same woman, how could she do this to me? She was like a rose: beautiful to see, sweet to smell, but the prick of thorns prevented me from touching her. To make matters worse, she was my client, so I had to work beside her, with every day a reminder of what I could not have.

In February of 1987, I wrote a letter to my friend Peggy in Phoenix, saying that the woman in question *was* the woman from the soulmate experience. Part of my letter said, "The happy part is I believe that my search for my soulmate is finally over; I think I have found her at last. The sad part is she wears a wedding ring."

In time, my anger cooled off into disappointment. I was sad, yes, but this time it was different. I had learned and grown from past experiences, and was much more mature. I had lived with five years of disappointment, and this was merely another. Was she the same woman of the soulmate experience? I wasn't positive, but I knew that exploring that question would only lead to more pain, so I avoided it. If I accepted her as my soulmate, it would be too painful for me to bear. Denial seemed like the only thing I could do. She can't be the one. I've got to stop thinking about her. Think about something else.

I buried my emotions under a pile of computer work, and I tried as hard as I could not to look into her eyes when I spoke with her, because I couldn't risk falling in love with her. Even so, I couldn't erase her from my mind.

Sometimes even now, when I close my eyes, I see her face as plain as day, like a photograph haunting my inner vision. There are times when I wish I could get her out of my mind, but I can't. She's like a ghost, haunting my mind yet impossible to hold. Although I never allowed myself to fall in love with her, every day I have to live with the thoughts of her, and what might have been. She may never know how I feel. Yet even from this, I learned. I grew.

> *"And so we end the chapter,*
> *And let the stage lights fade.*
> *I have seen you on the edge of dawn,*
> *Felt you here before you were born,*
> *Balanced your dreams upon the edge of thorns,*
> *But I don't think about you anymore."*
> —Savatage, "Edge of Thorns"

12

CATHYS AND KATHYS

Today I choose to celebrate the joy of my being.
Today I choose to look inward for that joy, not
outward.
Today I choose to see the outward as a reflection
of the inward.
Today I choose to give myself to the universe and
All That Is
and believe that the universe will fill all my needs.

—Inner Voice

A few months later, I tried to talk myself into believing that my soulmate was another woman somewhere else. With that thought in mind, I tried again to find her in an OBE on June 27, 1987.

I focused my mind in a completely passive way on a visualization of being weightless and standing upright. I continued to focus until it became real and I was out of my body. I got excited that the method worked, and my mind started to race. That eventually took me back to the body, and I had to start over.

Once again I focused my mind on the *feeling* of being weightless and upright. Within minutes I was once again out of my body. I found myself inside a home that I didn't recognize. At first I started to play with the feeling of weightlessness; I did several gravity-defying, playful acts like midair somersaults. I did this for a long time, perhaps ten minutes. I didn't want to explore the home; I just wanted to have fun with weightlessness and floating around. I walked out the front door to the sidewalk. The house I was in looked like many other homes in the area. The house was on the east side of the street. The street was typical of Rochester, Minnesota, with big overhanging trees on the boulevard blanketing the sidewalk with shade.

I started dancing down the sidewalk to the north, making giant leaps in the air because I was weightless. I did this several times and it was fun. Then I just started to glide through the air, with my feet off the ground.

I thought about what I wanted to do while out of the body. I thought about many possibilities, about visiting my mom or Peggy. Then I decided that I might have some luck trying to find my soulmate. I wondered what direction she was, but didn't have any clues. I thought, "I want to go where my soulmate is." As soon as that thought was firmly placed, my astral body twisted to the right and lifted up in the air above the trees. Very much to my surprise, I made a 180-degree turn, and started flying almost directly south.

I was surprised and started wondering where I was headed. Where could she be? . . . I didn't know how far I was going to travel, either. I was thinking of the possibilities when my mind somehow lost its focus and I found myself back in bed, lying down, in coincidence with my body. There was a blurry image in front of me, and I was curious what it was. I focused on the image and saw a bunch of circles with different dots in front of them. Some of the circles were blue and some were green, and the dots inside them were white, but there were other blue dots outside the image. The image seemed to be triangular. For a while I thought my mind was playing tricks on me. I focused on it very intently, and I was amazed that my consciousness was so clear and focused. Never before had astral vision been so complete and wonderful, yet I still couldn't identify the pattern I was seeing.

I decided to use analytical thinking and the left side of my brain, like an OBE I once had in which I saw an aloe plant but couldn't identify it properly.[12] I shifted my thinking to analytical mode, and thought intently, "Where have I seen that pattern before?" After a few minutes of thinking, I realized it was the pattern on certain portions of my bedspread. That's where I had seen it before, and that would explain why I was seeing it now; apparently some part of my bedspread was lying in front of my physical and astral eyes. I had never really studied the pattern of my bedspread before; I just always took it for granted and never had looked at the details.

With that mystery solved, I wondered what I should do next, and if I should continue the OBE. Then I decided that I had better chances of finding my soulmate out of the body than in. Since I was still out of the body, I decided to try again.

---

[12] The referenced OBE, from April 13, 1985, is described in chapter 19 of my *Out of Body Experiences*. In the OBE, I couldn't identify a peculiarly shaped aloe plant until I did math exercises in my head to engage the analytical side of my brain.

I refocused my mind on the floating-upright sensation again, to return to the original house. I found myself there, once more on the sidewalk. I faced south, floated myself up above it, and thought about my soulmate again. Once more, I started moving up and to the south. However, once again I lost my focus and came to on my bed. My body felt very heavy, and my mind was groggy. I rolled over to my right side and gave myself a few minutes for my consciousness to catch up with things, and to think about what had taken place.

When I rolled back to the original OBE position, I looked at my bedspread and saw the very same pattern in front of me. It was perfectly focused out of my body, but now that I was back in the body, the pattern was too close for my eyes to see.

Although Rochester was a great place to live, it didn't have any metaphysical discussion groups that I cared for. I had left my best friends in Phoenix, and I felt very isolated and lonely, so I decided to visit them—out of my body, of course. After all, why hop a plane to the coast when you can hop the astral plane to the "ghost?" This is what I did in July 1987:

At approximately 6:40 A.M., I was sleeping when I became conscious of my surroundings. I was in the bedroom of Cheri, the leader of my favorite discussion group in Phoenix, standing over her as she lay in bed. I looked at Cheri's body and was shocked to see how unhealthy she looked. I'm not sure if I was seeing her physical body or astral body, but regardless, it didn't look healthy. She looked strong, but not healthy. She looked like she was drained of energy and weak.

I placed my open-palmed hands about three inches above her midsection, and consciously poured energy from my hands into her.[13] I asked her how she was doing, and she said she was doing better. As always during OBEs, I'm sure it was her subconscious speaking. She spoke to me almost as if she were my patient, and I were one of her doctors.

Without warning my alarm clock rang, startling me half out of my wits.

I later found out that Cheri was dying of cancer. After she died, I kept visiting my friends. Although I missed them all, I kept thinking about Cathy.

I remember waking up to full consciousness, out of my body on December 20, 1987. In front of me was Peggy, my friend who lives in Phoenix. It had been almost a year since I had seen her last, and I was so overcome with joy at the sight of her that I hugged her like there was no tomorrow. I let go and took a step back. To my left was Patricia, another friend from Phoenix. Once again, I was overjoyed at seeing my dear friend, and I hugged Patricia. I let go and said something like, "God, I miss you so. I love you all very much." Then I noticed that behind Patricia stood another woman I didn't recognize. I turned back to Peggy, who was grinning. I asked her, "Where is Cathy?" but before she could respond, I lost consciousness. . . .

In 1989, I flew to Phoenix (this time in-the-body) to visit my friends. Over the course of a few days, Cathy and I spent a long time frolicking together in the woods of northern Arizona, talking, laughing, and holding hands. Her divorce was final, and she was a much more relaxed and confident woman. It seemed

---

[13] My T'ai Chi Chuan training had taught me how to manipulate my internal energy.

like we were a perfect pair. After I returned to Minnesota, we wrote long, romantic letters and talked for hours on the telephone every night. Finally, I asked her to move to Minnesota and live with me.

My relationship with Cathy was as much of a life-lesson as I'd ever had. It was one thing to deal with denied relationships and ideal relationship concepts. It was another thing all together to deal with a real live person.

When Cathy first arrived in Minnesota, everything seemed perfect. The universe put all the pieces together for us, as if this were meant to be. One of Cathy's favorite songs was "Orinoco Flow" by Enya, so it seemed like a message from the universe when we found a perfect house to rent in the nearby town of Oronoco, Minnesota. The rent was very cheap, the house was on a lake, and to top if off, our landlord's last name was Love. It seemed the universe had guided us to our perfect place.

I introduced Cathy to some of my friends and co-workers: Kathy Jacobs and her husband, Bruce; Kathy Melberg; and a few others. We all had one thing in common: we were stuck in Rochester, Minnesota. Together, we went camping, had parties, and sat up late at night having philosophical discussions.

It wasn't long, however, before things started going wrong in my relationship with Cathy. Because Cathy's dad had left her when she was a girl, she had never seen a positive male-female relationship when she was growing up. As an adult, she was badly hurt by her ex-husband who cheated on her and did drugs behind her back. She didn't like or trust men, because they had always hurt her. Since I was a man, she didn't trust me either.

I had my own problems. I was very inexperienced in relationships, so I didn't have some of the basic skills

I needed. I thought that the only things I needed were love, patience, and willingness to learn. I was wrong. It's funny how our society feeds us useless physical knowledge for twelve years of our lives, but doesn't give us any of the skills we most need to deal with life, like relationship skills.

My relationship with Cathy suffered many problems. She seemed to misunderstand everything I said and did. There were countless times when she would interpret every sentence I said in a negative way. Even when I was being positive, she would question my motives and not trust what I was saying. The truth of the matter was that we couldn't communicate with each other. She was emotional, artistic, and right-brained, whereas I was intellectual, analytical, and left-brained.

She blamed me for all the problems in our relationship, and I blamed myself too. It became obvious that I couldn't do anything right in her eyes. I tried everything I could to save our relationship, including regular visits to a marriage counselor (we weren't even married), but everything I tried failed. I tried to become the person she wanted, but that was the fatal mistake. She told me countless times that I was being selfish, and so I tried to sacrifice myself for the sake of the relationship. I sold my Harley and gave up my hobbies. I gave up my OBE practice time, too, and devoted myself entirely to the relationship and to being a parent to Cathy's daughter.

Eventually I learned that sacrificing who you are creates only resentment, so it's better to just be yourself. Nothing is worth sacrificing your self. If your partner doesn't love you for who you are, you can't change that fact. You can't make anyone love you. I learned that an important part of a loving relationship is to love and accept yourself. Self-esteem is one of the most important qualities you can have. I learned that you can never change another person; he or she has to want to change first. You can, however, change yourself, and that's exactly what I did. I decided to be more social, so I joined a company-sponsored volleyball team. I decided to improve my relationship skills, so I enrolled in several community education classes. One class was on interpersonal communication, and another was on creative expression and showing emotions.

Another class was on loving relationships, offered by a doctor from Rochester's Mayo Clinic. He gave several pages of "do" and "don't" tips for relationships. Here are some of his tips:

> Listen to your partner. Don't interrupt them when they're speaking; just shut up and listen. Learn nondefensive listening. Look at the person you're talking with. Watch their body language. Clarify what the other person is saying. Repeat back (paraphrase) what you heard. "It seems to me that you're saying . . ." Try to understand your partner's feelings. Try to draw out their feelings. "How did you feel when . . . ?" Give them feedback. Try not to get defensive. It's better to ask than to assume that you're being blamed. "Are you blaming me for . . . ?"

> Avoid blame statements. Avoid "you are" statements. It's not fair to say, "You're feeling this way." It's better to use your interpretation, for example, "You look angry." Avoid words like "should," "ought," and "must." "You should feel" is doubly unfair.

Use plenty of "I feel" statements. "I feel as if you're blaming me." State your feelings and the cause. "I feel angry because you didn't do the dishes." Give yourself time to feel your feelings and take time to examine your feelings. Give your partner time and space to "feel" their feelings too. Respect your partner. Treat them with high regard.

I also read a number of books on relationships. One was *His Needs, Her Needs* (Harley 1986), and it was a real eye-opener. I learned that everyone has needs in a relationship, and that men's needs are different from women's needs. Harley said that it's important to understand your needs in a relationship, and although needs will be different from person to person, most men typically have the same five needs, and most women typically have the same five needs. For women he listed affection, conversation, honesty and openness, financial support, and family commitment (in that order). For men he listed sexual fulfillment, recreational companionship, an attractive spouse, domestic support, and admiration (in that order).

I tried to understand my needs, but my needs didn't fit either of these columns. My needs were a mixture of both lists.

I struggled month after month to save my relationship with Cathy, but nothing worked. Everything I did was met with hostility. The only person I felt comfortable enough to share this with was Kathy Melberg, who was on my volleyball team and had been my friend for years. Kathy was also a computer programmer, analytical and primarily left-brained, so we were very comfortable with each other and could communicate well.

After struggling for over a year, it was clear to me that Cathy didn't love me and was incapable of fulfilling my needs in a relationship. If your partner won't meet your basic needs, then you shouldn't be in the relationship. So I had to end my relationship with Cathy because no relationship is worth sacrificing your needs. You can sacrifice wants, but not needs. I found out that it's important to be with someone who accepts you and loves you *as you are*. It's important to be with someone you can communicate with, and who makes you feel comfortable.

After I broke up with Cathy, I was frustrated and angry. I vowed to be more cautious in my relationships, and I vowed to never sacrifice my "self" for anyone else. I read a wonderful book called *I Deserve Love* by Sondra Ray. That small book taught me a great deal about the power of affirmations and petitioning the universe to get what you want. In June 1989, I made a list of all the qualities I wanted, even demanded, in a mate. It was a bitter, six-page list that encompassed every way Cathy had ever hurt me. Then one day during lunch break, I sat on the sidelines of a ping-pong game between Kathy Melberg and another programmer. As I watched, I mentally amended my list of demands. I thought, "I've had enough of one-sided relationships. I want someone who loves me. Someone who is fun and happy." As I watched, I found my eyes following Kathy Melberg as she swayed to the rhythm of her ping-pong game. She was such a good friend. I found myself thinking, "Someone I can talk with comfortably. Someone like . . ." My eyes scanned her up and down. "Kathy Melberg."

Months later, on October 10, 1989, our little circle

of friends (minus Cathy) went out to dinner together at the Tick-Tock Café, a tiny hole-in-the-wall restaurant that was owned by an outstanding Belgian chef named Franz. It was the best-kept secret in Rochester. After dinner, Kathy and I started talking. We got into her car and drove south to the deserted Forestville State Park, where we walked in the moonlight, held hands, and talked. The crisp Minnesota autumn night started turning cold, so we lit a fire in the shelter's fireplace and kept talking.

As the months went by, Kathy and I spent more time together. We grew closer and fell deeply, permanently, in love. My search for my soulmate was over. I hadn't found what I expected but I had found something much more important: a loving relationship with a completely compatible person, and now I had the skills to make it last forever. More importantly, I was free to be me once again, and I promptly resumed my OBE practice.

In May of 1992, Kathy and I were married, and we've been joyfully married since then. We live together, drive to work together, and write computer programs side by side in the same office of a small high-tech company. We spend twenty-four hours a day together, and our relationship is better than I ever dreamed. We have a special friendship, intimacy, and closeness that I never dreamed possible.

So what about the mentor I once knew and the haunted memories of a soulmate? Perhaps it was all just a big life-lesson like Peggy's gift. Or maybe she was someone special from a distant past life, or maybe she has a place in some alternate reality. In any case, it doesn't diminish my love for Kathy now, nor will it ever. I'm totally convinced that Kathy and I planned to share our love together long before we were born, and in that sense, we are soulmates. Here's the cool part: the first day I met Kathy was in October 1987, which is precisely when the Ouija board said I would meet my soulmate.

While it may be possible for soulmates to find each other during an out-of-body experience, developing a loving relationship demands a lot of in-the-body work as well. Learning to listen (paying attention) and learning to communicate (showing your feelings) are two of the most important parts of a loving relationship, and it is something I had to learn the hard way.

13

A PARTING GIFT

"What's today's lesson?" I asked my inner voice.
"Today, imagine that you only have five days left
to live.
What do you still need to accomplish? Do you
need to forgive someone?
Do you need to tell someone you love them? And
so on."

On September 26, 1987, I had another unusual lesson. It was one of those pie-in-the-face lessons, and it taught me a great deal.

I was cleaning up some broken bottles in the basement of an old building and I had cut my hand on the glass. The cut didn't look bad, but the glass was wet with some unknown liquid, so I decided to see a doctor anyway. After a short examination and blood test, the doctor told me that the liquid was a type of poison, and that I would die soon. He couldn't tell me how long I had to live—a minute or a month—but I would surely die from that cut.

As I left the doctor and walked back home, my mind raced. First I thought about what I would do in my last moments. I decided that there wasn't enough time left to do anything "significant." Then I realized that the really "significant" things in life are the little things and not the big ones.

I felt regret that I couldn't do all the things I wanted to do in life—not the big things, but the little ones. It didn't matter that I never took that big trip to Europe, but I felt disappointed because of all the little things I had decided to pass by, like the books that sat on my shelf while I had no ambition to read. I felt disappointed because I had so many opportunities to touch people's lives with joy, but I passed so many of those opportunities by. I felt disappointed for all the times I told myself, "There will be another time to do these things." My time was running out.

There was no fear. None.

I accepted the fact that I would soon die. Crying, wailing, moaning, and worrying wouldn't do me or anyone any good. What would happen to me when I died? I decided it didn't matter. After all, I would find out soon enough, and all the conjecture in the world wouldn't change that fact.

I thought about my friends. What would they do without me? I decided that it didn't matter, because they had no choice but to go on without me. Would they miss me? I realized that if they decided to miss me, that was their choice, and I couldn't help that. Can I ease their loss or pain over my death? I decided I couldn't because they chose their own emotions. I wouldn't want them to be sad because of me, but if they were, only they could change that fact. What did they think of my life and my life's accomplishments? I decided that my friends had already formed their opinions of me, and my current condition shouldn't change that—it's the life and not the death that makes the man. I decided that my accomplishments weren't nearly as important as who I was inside. I realized that nothing had changed. We always face the possibility of death, every moment we're alive. It's just that few of us look at the issue until it's too late. Most of us take a long, healthy life for granted, until it gets snatched away unexpectedly.

Finally, I embraced the possibility of my death wholeheartedly. I realized that I was creating my reality at that very moment, just as I had always created it in the past. Since I was creating my reality, I decided to live my life to the fullest, right up until the end. I knew I could even choose not to die, but should I? Since I had accepted my death, I decided to leave that decision up to my oversoul and peacefully accept what came.

So I went about my day as if nothing were wrong. After three or so hours, all my friends had found out that I had been poisoned. They seemed depressed and they didn't know how to handle it. It seemed pretty strange to me—after all, it was *my* death, my body, my moment of truth, my problem, and not theirs.

A few people approached me about my death. Most of the people who approached me were speechless. What could they say? What should they say? What could I say to them?

Most of them said nothing, but they sent me a message anyway: "I want to share this moment with you, to be close to you one last time. To tell you that I care. Even if I never said it before, I do love you." A few tried to tell me they were sorry. For what? For my decision? After all, my passing from this life would be a rebirth into a glorious new life. I didn't even question that fact.

I joined my friends for dinner. I didn't think about it as my last meal; I didn't think about death at all, but about life. I didn't think about when I would die, but about how much more of life I would allow myself to enjoy. When we were done with supper, we all talked and laughed while we were getting up from the table.

I felt a little bit funny. I stopped walking and my friends all stared at me, waiting, wondering. They all stopped talking and suddenly the room became quiet. I could hear and feel my heart beating. Thump, thump, thump. Suddenly there was a "click" and silence. My heart had stopped. I wasn't afraid. I wasn't in pain. I didn't panic. I tried to think quickly. What should I do? What final message can I give these people?

I felt very weak but there was no pain at all. I started to fall backward but someone caught me and set me gently on the cold floor.

Then all hell broke loose, with people shouting and running around. They seemed panic-stricken. I was calm. They seemed terrified. I was sure. They seemed sad. I was happy. My body started to feel numb, and I started losing control of it. Quick! What can I give them? They all cared for me so much. What gift can I leave them with?

I was dying. Nothing physical is really important because someday you have to leave it behind. I decided the only important thing in life is what we get out of it, the messages, the truths, the wisdom, the learning, the fun. What was the most important of these messages? Love.

I tried to say it, "Love," but the message came out garbled, and there was too much noise, confusion, and panic in the room. God damn it, anyway, this is important! "Love." "Love." "Love!" At last, the cherished word choked out of my dying body, but I wasn't sure that they heard or understood.

I struggled to gain more control over the body, but it was useless. As the people tried to convince my heart to beat again, vibrations swept over me, and I gently slipped out of body. This part was not new; I had slipped out of my body hundreds of times before.

Now the crowd didn't seem concerned with me; they were only concerned with that body that was lying on the floor. I realized that body had once housed me. What a concept. I felt like a camper watching his tent get destroyed from outside of it. I decided I couldn't do anything to help the crowd now, it was all up to them. It was over for me.

I watched them work on my body for a while, then I got bored with it all and left. I suddenly realized that my friends and I were a special spiritual task force for the Earth.

Somehow, I knew that there had also been a wonderful, silent astral counterpart to our group. They worked toward the same goal of spirituality, but from the Other Side. Even though I had never known it before, our two teams worked side by side, hand in hand. I decided that my next step should be to meet these people, and perhaps join their forces. I changed my frequency so that I would move toward their building.

I left my old friends to fend for themselves. No, I wasn't leaving them; I could never leave them. I was going to be with them. I would watch over them, protect them, and help them in our common goal. I would always be at their sides. I reached the door of the counterpart building, and I paused.

I felt happy because I was indeed alive, not dead. I felt happy because it was over; a man who is dead is indestructible. I felt happy because I didn't have to leave my friends. I could still be with them. I could still work with them, love them, help them, and watch their lives unfold. I could still send them my love, although in more subtle ways. I had the rest of eternity to regain all of those lost opportunities. Most importantly, I had given them my gift. One word: "Love." I hadn't entered death, I had entered life. . . .

The dream ended and I woke up. Imagine my surprise when I found out I was still alive. The sun was shining and birds were chirping outside. Such a glorious new day. I was always told that if you died in your dreams, you would die in real life. Now I know that is definitely a myth. Death had been so wonderful, I'd like to do it again some time.

14

HELPING

"What's today's lesson?" I asked my inner voice.
"Today, give your service unselfishly."

In mid-May 1996, Kathy and I had both been in Rochester for more than nine years, and we were getting tired of the daily routine. We decided to move back to Minneapolis to be closer to our families, and began sending out resumes and interviewing with prospective employers. The task of job-hunting was a relatively new experience for me, because I had never *found* a job before. Up to that point, perfect computer jobs always found *me* through long and humorously complex series of coincidences, and hints from my inner voice.

On one occasion, Kathy and I took a day off from work to drive to Minneapolis for some event and Kathy scheduled a job interview for the afternoon. I didn't know how long Kathy's interview would last, so rather than waiting in the car, I opted to spend the afternoon at Southdale Mall, which was nearby.

Once inside the mall, I noticed there were very few people there. I didn't feel much like shopping, so I decided to have some fun. As I calmed my mind and tried to raise my vibrations, a strange tingling sensation came over me. The tingling went up my spine and out through the top of my head, and I felt strangely empowered. In the past, that sensation always meant something important was happening.

I decided to follow my intuition. "Let's have some fun. Which way should I go?" I playfully asked my inner voice. I could feel my inner voice grinning at me mischievously, giving me a gentle "Let's go this way," but instead of starting a dialogue with my inner voice in the usual way, I just closed my eyes and let my guidance take me in any direction. Automatically following my inner guidance, I walked forward several steps, turned sharply to the right, and strolled down a particularly deserted hallway in the mall. I occasionally opened my eyes to make sure I wasn't going to bump into anything.

When I reached the end of the hall, I opened my eyes again and looked around. At my feet, there was a man lying on the ground, and he wasn't breathing. "Oh my God," I thought, "what should I do? This man is dying, and I don't have any medical training and I don't know CPR."

The first thing I did was run to a nearby store and tell the store clerk, "Call the paramedics down here now!" Then I ran back to the man to see what I could do to help. The man's right hand was moving slowly and his eyes were moving, so I knew he was still alive, but he still wasn't breathing. I looked around on the ground, and noticed a small bottle-like object lying next to the man: It was some kind of inhaler like those used by asthma patients. Now I knew what was happening: the man had had an attack of asthma and that's why he couldn't breathe. I didn't have a clue how to use the inhaler, so I stuck the thing in his mouth and pressed down on the button, releasing a small spray on the man's tongue.

By this time a nearby store clerk came over to watch, and she said that the inhaler spray probably needed to reach his lungs and that the spray on his tongue wouldn't be good enough. So I stuck the inhaler deeper inside the man's mouth, covered the rest of his mouth, and sprayed the medication down his throat once more, trying to avoid the tongue. Then I set the inhaler down on the ground, squatted next to the man, held my open palms over the man's chest, and started summoning the tingling energy I felt earlier.

At once, a stream of energy started flowing through my body, through my palms, and into the man's body. Readers of my first book may recall an incident (described in chapter 15) where I discovered I could astrally heal by programming people's brains. Now I was called upon to do it physically, not astrally. I tried to put a portion of my consciousness inside the man's head and then used visualization to "see" the white spheres of light inside the man's brain. Then I tried to consciously "tell" his brain, "Breathe again, dammit." What's keeping those paramedics? I wondered. I tried to psychically command his heart to continue pumping. "Pump, dammit."

A minute or so later, two paramedics came rushing through the hallway with their medical bags in hand. When they reached the man, I stopped the flow of energy from my hands, stood up, and let them do their job. At once, they started checking the man's vital statistics and administered the care he needed.

As I walked away, my body was bristling with an inner fire that stayed with me until late into the evening. I tried to shop for a few minutes, but I was too pumped up with a mixture of adrenaline and psychic energy, so I went back to check on the man. He was breathing again and talking with the paramedics. A few minutes later, he was sitting up, obviously feeling much better. I thought about born-again Christians and wondered how they can claim that psychic abilities and the inner voice are tricks of Satan. Then I wondered why my inner voice had not given me more of a sense of urgency, but I realized that would have interfered more than helped me in finding the man.

I never spoke to the man. It was enough to know that he was all right, and that I probably saved his life. When Kathy picked me up, she told me all about her interview, then she asked me what I did all afternoon. "Not much," I replied calmly, "I wandered around the mall . . . did some shopping . . . saved a man's life." "What?" Kathy made me tell the whole story.

"So you're a hero," she said afterward. "No," I replied, "I'm no hero. My brother Tom is a fireman and he's saved a lot more lives than I ever have or ever will. He's the hero of the family." "But you never even gave that guy a chance to thank you." "I don't want any thanks. Helping people is enough reward; besides, he probably didn't even know I helped him."

"*He knew*," my inner voice said to me in a voice Kathy could not hear.

15

THE TEST

"What's today's lesson?" I asked my inner voice.
"Today, wherever you go, imagine that you are
surrounded by angels who help you, guide you,
*   and protect you.*
They are really there, you know."

After getting a job and moving back to Minneapolis in October of 1996, I felt like I was back where I belonged. Once again, I resumed my OBE experiments. This time I was more daring. Calling for astral helpers usually works well; I've felt their gentle hands helping to tug me away from my body. The strange thing is that I rarely see these helpers. Perhaps they're usually invisible because their vibrations are so much higher than mine. Here is part of an OBE from May 1999.

Kathy and I were at her mom's cabin in northern Minnesota. After Kathy got up this morning, I decided to do some OBE stuff. I'd been reading Sophy Burnham's book *The Ecstatic Journey* and it made me want a transcendental God experience. I figured an OBE would be the perfect way to try it. I began to focus on swaying. I went deeper and deeper until I started getting hypnagogic images. One image was of a building, so I started focusing on the image of the building to the exclusion of everything else. As the image became clear, the swaying increased. The buzzing began, and I whooshed up and out of my body.

My first thought/intent was "I want to experience God, enlightenment, etc.," but I didn't know exactly how to do that. My first attempt was an appeal to my oversoul/higher self or to any invisible entities who might be with me, and to God, but nothing happened.

So I started focusing on raising my vibrations, and as I did, I started floating up into the air. It was a beautiful, warm, spring day and the air smelled sweet and fresh. I felt alive, and I kept floating up. My heart filled with joy and love and I felt no restrictions, no limitations, no gravity. There was absolute clarity. I was very conscious, very aware, very alive.

Joyously, I whooshed from one faraway place to the next. With my newfound freedom, I whooshed into Minneapolis buildings (seventy-five miles from the cabin), through them, and out the other side. I whooshed into residential areas, whooshing into people's houses and right through them. I remember pausing at the top of someone's wall near a vaulted ceiling. I looked down to see the occupants inside. Then I whooshed on again.

At some point, I stopped and thought, "Too bad the government won't pay me to do OBE work. I could spy on people, look for drug dealers or what not. I can fly into any home and any building. This is great!"

I whooshed through the side of an apartment building, and down through the hallway. I whooshed downstairs and saw a woman leaving the apartment building through the front door, and I whooshed right past her, passing her on her right side. Then I stopped and stood on the grass outside, looking at the beautiful spring day.

I believe that we are constantly surrounded by angels/astral helpers who are willing to assist us in our spiritual growth, whether we are in or out of the body. In my OBEs they are almost always invisible. Many times, I've felt their gentle hands helping me out of my body after I had induced the proper state. Now I appealed to one of these invisible helpers for a Christ-consciousness experience, but nothing happened. Then suddenly my heart was filled with joy and I rose up into the sky. As I did, I thought about the problems I used to have with flying when I first started having OBEs (described in my first book, *Out of Body Experiences*). I also wondered why I wasn't getting a "God" experience. Then I heard a voice say, "First you must fully realize your freedom."

As I continued to rise into the sky, I thought about my "master" experience (see chapter 4) in which I was taken to a high church steeple and I understood that a major step in my spiritual progress would be to jump from that height with total confidence. That was the freedom the voice spoke about. The freedom from "what ifs" and fear. As long as I held on to my doubts, I wouldn't be free enough to experience God. I would be tethered by my own self-imposed leash. I needed to let go. I vowed to work on it.

By now, I was several thousand feet in the air and I stopped and let myself drop with total confidence. I whooshed to the ground, flying joyously once more. There were no doubts or fears. When I landed, I didn't know where I was. Was it some unfamiliar part of

Minneapolis or a different city? I broadcasted a thought to these helpers, "Okay, I want to learn my freedom."

Just then, an invisible helper gently took hold of my feet. I was pulled backward by my feet, then lifted tens of thousands of feet into the sky, feet up and head down. Although I was hanging by my feet at least twice as high as the average passenger jet, I wasn't afraid; I was playful. "Sure. Now you're going to just drop me, right?" I joked toward the helper. And it did! Head down, I started plunging to the Earth at high speed. Ironically, I remembered an obscure song, "High Speed Dirt," by the heavy-metal group Megadeth:

> *Do it if you dare, Leaping from the sky*
> *Hurling thru the air, Exhilarating high*
> *See the Earth below, Soon to make a crater*
> *Blue sky, black death, I'm off to meet my maker!*

There was no fear; I was completely confident.

Then, as I plunged, I wondered if I had been away from my body too long. As I thought of my body, I was refocused there and came to. I didn't end the OBE out of fear. I passed the test.

16

CHASING GOD

"What's today's lesson?" I asked my inner voice.
"Today, whenever you see someone, think to
*   yourself,*
'I bless you in the name of God.'
Acknowledge and encourage the divine in them,
and claim the divinity in you."

Some people may classify OBEs as "religious experiences,"[14] but I assure you that out-of-body experiences can be as diverse as in-the-body experiences, and therefore are not necessarily religious in nature. If you want to do less-than-noble things like watch the girl next door take off her clothes, there's nothing stopping you. (Note, however, that it would be difficult to do because your desire and low vibrations are most likely enough to keep you inside your body.) OBEs usually require a certain amount of control over your mind. Often you need to raise your vibrations to

---

[14]Some of the world's great religions and myths may be based on out-of-body experiences. See chapter 20 for more details.

achieve the experience; therefore, it's easier to have a spiritual OBE than a nonspiritual OBE.

It's also easier to induce religious experiences out of your body than inside your body. Religious experience is a natural, profound and deeply moving use of OBEs. Here is a journal entry from my first religious OBE, dated May 1996:

When I went to bed, I was wide awake and couldn't sleep at first. At home, I was lying on my right side on the waterbed. For no particular reason, I started thinking about Jesus Christ and God, and wondering about Christ's relationship to God. It was probably because I had started reading a book that deals with this topic. As I was lying there immobile, I started focusing my mind in OBE fashion, but instead of visualizing an ordinary image, I held the image of Christ in my mind, plus an icon that I used to represent God. The image of Christ was on the left side of my visual field, and the icon of God was on the right side. As my mind focused into the OBE state, I had the passing thought, "No, Jesus should be at the right hand of the Father." Then I realized that "right" and "left" are relative to "forward" and "backward," and since I believed that God was everywhere, comprising all that is, God didn't have a forward or backward. I decided it didn't matter if Christ was to the left or right of my icon of God.

As I pulled myself down into the OBE state, my image of Christ seemed to become very real, and so did the icon or idea of God. It seemed as if I actually felt the presence of Jesus Christ, and through Jesus, a connection with God. Now, I'm not a very religious man outwardly, so this is very much out of the ordinary for me. It seemed as if Christ were helping me, sending me his love.

I started to swing my consciousness forward and backward in my usual fashion, and tried to maintain that crucial state of single-minded focus, but as I rocked, I could feel the presence of Christ, and that distracted my mind. I tried to swing away from my body in a forceful motion, but I didn't have enough momentum built up yet; therefore I swung back and hit the body, which made me go back to the normal in-the-body state.

I've occasionally been accosted by born-again Christians who consider my OBEs the work of the Devil. What they don't realize is that they can use OBEs to meet Jesus Christ firsthand rather than thinking about him abstractly. Another attempt at a religious OBE (in January 1997) yielded interesting results:

Kathy and I were at Kathy's parents' cabin with some friends. In the midafternoon, I lay down to attempt an OBE. I induced the trance, but couldn't sit up, even though I was separate from my body. I struggled a while, then came back.

I decided to try again, so without moving my body, I immediately tried to induce an OBE again. My consciousness was pretty clear. I used a relatively new method that involved intensely imagining that my body was swaying back and forth, swiveling my hips, as if I were standing up and shifting my weight from foot to foot repeatedly. The method worked, and within minutes, I was free from my body again. I made a mental note that I should use this in the future as a method of teaching OBEs.

As soon as I got out, I said, "Yes!" and thought about what I wanted to do. Once again, I tried to sit up, and was unable to do so. I struggled a while, then came out of it again.

I induced the OBE again, reached my arms out in front of me, and opened my eyes. I couldn't see my arms, so I knew I was out-of-body for sure. This time I decided to try to contact God.

I stood up, this time successfully. I looked up to the heavens and prayed. I said something like, "God, Almighty, Creator of all things, I reach out for you." As I said that, I reached up toward the sky with my mind. My soul became charged with energy, and I felt my aura expand in rings of energy out from my astral body.

My energy rose, and reached up to the sky higher and higher. Almost at once, a single bolt of energy came shooting down from above and hit me. The force of the energy bolt was so powerful that it knocked my astral body to the ground. It was just raw power; there was no feeling behind it. I lay there stunned for a second, wondering why I didn't encounter something more religious or loving or holy. Then I came back to my body again. I didn't feel I was being punished at all; it was more like I had touched an energy force too powerful for me to handle.

This religious OBE had even more interesting results, in June 1999. This morning I got up at my usual time of 5:45 A.M., put the dogs out, and drank a can of caffeinated Surge soda pop to get motivated.[15] Then I worked on the computer for an hour. I went back to bed around 7:00 A.M. After Kathy got up, I decided to do an OBE. I tried to induce an OBE but instead I fell asleep. I woke up around 8:00 A.M. and decided to try again. I tried for about ten minutes, then I got restless. I decided

---

[15]Some authors claim that stimulants like caffeine inhibit your ability to induce OBEs, but I've never had a problem.

I'd give it one more shot, and if I weren't successful, I'd get up.

So I rolled onto my back and gave it my best shot. I didn't think I'd be successful, but much to my surprise, I was able to coax my mind down into the proper state easily from that point. I waved myself out as normal. Once I was out, I pushed myself forward, through the bedroom wall until I was hanging in midair between our house and my neighbor's house.

I knew exactly what I wanted to do. At once, I made my request to no one in particular, saying, "I want to experience God." Suddenly, I was transported to some place that looked like outer space. In the blackness of space in front of me was an image of a single human eye, and it was white against the black background. I focused on the image of the eye, and saw that it comprised tiny pinpoints of light. If this were part of a face, I wondered, why didn't I see any other features?

I decided to pan backward so I could see more of the image. What I saw astounded me. As I panned back, I saw that the pinpoints of light were slowly swirling around the eye: What I was looking at was not an eye, but a galaxy. The "eye" was actually a cluster of stars in the center of the galaxy. I continued to pan back, and the image of the galaxy started getting smaller. "Whoa!" I thought, "Where the hell am I?" Instantly, I lost consciousness and began dreaming. If I had remained calm, would I have continued to pan outward until I experienced the totality of All That Is?

Here is another OBE where I tried to contact God. This journal entry is from February 20, 2000:

This morning I tried to induce an OBE around 9:00 A.M., and was successful. After careful consideration, I decided to try once more to contact God. I reached out with my mind with the intent of experiencing God and something strange happened. I was staring at the ceiling of my bedroom, and I noticed a spider crawling on the ceiling. Somehow, I knew this was another test as a second, third, and fourth spider converged on the ceiling. Who or what was giving me this test?

Soon there were dozens of spiders on the ceiling above me. I realized I wasn't really seeing spiders, I was seeing the illusion of spiders as part of the test. I also realized what the test was: before I could realize oneness with God, I had to embrace and experience God's love. I had to raise my vibrations to the level of God. I reasoned that God loves all things, even spiders and the most hideous creatures on the planet. How could I expect to attain oneness with God until I raised my own love to that same level? Spiders were just the first question of the exam.

I suddenly became very emotional and pleaded my answer to the invisible helper who gave me the test, "Yes, I will love all things, even the spiders," but I knew the test was not over: my ability (or inability) to love would be pushed far beyond my endurance, and that's why I was so overcome with emotions. This was just the beginning; what other horrors would I have to face, and love? I was overcome with emotions and started sobbing until I was reintegrated with my body. I opened my eyes and thought about the OBE a long time before getting up.

So far, my attempts to contact God in an OBE have yielded some interesting results, but not the results I wanted. Other people, however, have been successful. The following is one such religious OBE submitted by Christopher Hazlitt, who insists, "If you travel far enough, you will meet yourself." He writes:

One warm afternoon in 1996 I took a short nap. I awoke within it to find myself standing in the presence of a huge sun or sphere of light and I quickly learned that this sun was pure consciousness and awareness. Although its surface was only swirling light and did not have a face, it seemed as if it was smiling at me and had nothing but love for me. I felt its thoughts as one with my own and felt it peering deeply into my own awareness, knowing everything about me all at once. Standing in its presence I was overcome by a deep sense of awe and at the same time I was surprised to find myself so fully conscious in this light-filled void. There was nothing in existence for me but myself and this sun smiling its awareness at me. It was unlike any place on Earth, and yet as real as waking reality. In fact, it was more real; I was super-conscious. Suddenly I came to a profound awareness that this sun was God!

I was so overwhelmed and surprised that God was real that I gasped and then yelled out, "You're real!"

I had always had a deep mistrust of religion. Years before this experience, I had decided for many seemingly valid reasons that religion and God were only a product of the human mind, yet there I was standing in the presence of what I knew without a doubt was God. What I had previously thought to be the truth about the universe was shattered and I stood there stunned, having had my world turned around so quickly. I was happy because I had always hoped that God was real and that there was a future beyond the physical. As I stood in its presence, I perceived myself to be nothing but pure awareness and without a body. This

"Sun of Awareness" fully merged with me, seeing everything inside of me. It saw everything I had ever done (and failed to do) both good and bad, and yet I did not sense or feel this being was judging me or my past. There was no serial or motion picture-like review of my life, just a sudden and full knowing about all things I have ever done, thought, and experienced.

Because this Sun of Awareness/God was peering so fully and deeply into me, I felt totally naked, more naked than if I were standing without clothes in front of a million people. This being seemed to be the consciousness of everyone I had ever known plus that of millions of others. It seemed to be everyone, but incredible as it might seem, most of all it seemed to be me. Even though I had no awareness of having a body, this feeling of nakedness was more than I could stand. Before I had time to think about what I was doing, I began moving away from this being as fast as I could. It wasn't that I was afraid, nor that I wanted to get away from this wonderful sun of light; it was more like an automatic response to feeling more naked than I thought "naked" could be.

As I was traveling away from this being I found myself bursting through some kind of barrier into a blackness that was filled with wonderful stars. As I continued moving forward at a tremendous speed through the star fields, I soon found myself slowing down as if I was up against another barrier or membrane. It seemed to stretch slightly and then I burst through it into another blackness of star-filled space. I continued to speed away faster and faster, but regardless of how much physical distance I traveled, I was never any farther away from the Sun of Awareness at all.

I quickly traveled through several star-filled spaces, each separated from one another by barriers that I was easily penetrating. It seemed as if the farther I got from the sphere of light, the smaller I got and the more divided I became. As I passed through each layer its consciousness was still with me, even though my speed increased. It was still deeply within my consciousness. All of a sudden, I fell through the top of my bedroom ceiling, hit my body with a jolt, and immediately woke up. The jolt was so strong that my bed physically bounced as my body jerked awake in response to the sudden stop.

I opened my eyes and immediately spoke in a low and powerful voice, "I am that great I am." I said this almost involuntarily; the words spilled out of my mouth without even thinking about what or why I was saying it. I also knew what this meant: that I was the very consciousness that I was trying to get away from!

As much as I tried to get away from the Sun of Awareness, I could never get one fraction of an inch farther away from it, no matter how far or fast I traveled. Even after waking up, it was still with me. To this day, I still feel and know its presence. I believe that this Sun of Awareness/God wasn't a single being, but is the center of all beings, that it is me, you, and perhaps all conscious beings. From this experience, I think that somewhere at the center of each of us is a spark of this same light, and without it we would not have consciousness, and perhaps without us it would not exist either.

Because of this experience, I came to see everyone around me as myself. At the same time, I also saw this as equally true from everyone else's perspective: that I am them, too. They too can look around and only see other parts of themselves, other selves experiencing life from another point of view, separated by their physical bodies, by their individual minds and wills, but in reality they are one at their core.

These feelings and thoughts were so strong that I had trouble referring to other people at work as anything other than "I." I had a tendency to think about others as just another part of myself. Just as I think about my hands as being a part of me, I would sometimes refer to others as "I" instead of the name of the person. For example, instead of saying, "He had finished doing that paperwork," it came out as "I had finished doing that paperwork." I had to relearn how to refer to others as separate from myself. After four years, I still think of others as myself, but now I can stop myself from verbalizing it.

If I had the chance to do it over again and stand in the presence of this Sun of Awareness/God, I wouldn't run away from it no matter how startling it is to be seen to such depth. I now hope that I would stand in its presence no matter how naked I felt. I don't believe that my motive for running was because I couldn't stand to face the light, or that I felt like a bad person, but because I was so unaccustomed to being seen so fully, so suddenly, so clearly, and to such depth. Unfortunately, my flight away from it took place before I could think of what I was doing and why.

The words I spoke after the experience, "I am that great I am," meant that, although I am individual here, I am also a part of every other consciousness at the great central point of consciousness: God. I am now secure in the knowledge that this presence of consciousness has always been with me, and that I have never been alone and never will be. I now know that this presence is closer to me than anything else in the universe. I had been so accustomed to it that I didn't know it was there, much like becoming used to a smell in a room. Once you are there with it long enough, it begins to fade into the background. Like silence, it is always there, maybe in the background, behind and between the sounds, but always there.

I'll continue to experiment with religious experiences, and who knows what I'll find.

17

THE OBE OUTLOOK ON LIFE

"What's today's lesson?" I asked my inner voice.
"Today, give yourself permission to be who you
*   are.*
After you've done that, give yourself permission
*   to be*
who you most want to be. Suspend the disbelief
*   of yourself."*

There are a lot of good uses for out-of-body experiences. Solving crimes and finding missing children are good applications. Astronomers can use OBEs to explore the vast reaches of outer space. Oceanographers can use it to explore the depths of the oceans. Physicists can use it to explore the smallest subatomic particles, which could lead to new theories regarding the origins of physical matter, energy, and nonphysical realities. Some people claim that the United States government is already using controlled remote viewing for spying. Perhaps some day, FBI, CIA, and NSA forces will have teams of astral travelers dedicated to reconnaissance. Maybe they're already using the OBE technique but not telling us.

The most important application for OBE is to further our spiritual growth. With it, we can learn about ourselves, such as who we are and why we are here in this physical world. We can use it to explore the afterlife, or to learn the true nature of God, or to learn the deeper meanings in our lives. My OBEs have changed my outlook on daily life. They've taught me to view life through a new perspective, a perspective based on nonphysical life rather than physical life.

Life Is a School

A good writer doesn't waste words. Every sentence has an important meaning and implication toward the outcome of the book. Likewise, a good movie or television show doesn't have any wasted scenes. Every scene has a bearing on the outcome of the movie, and usually every "minor incident" has an implication of something greater in the story. And so it is with life. I believe we are all actors and actresses on the stage of life. We are temporary visitors to this planet, passing through this world on a very short journey. We're here to learn, to teach, and to grow spiritually through experiences. When we are asleep, we spend hours writing and rewriting the screenplay and creating the scripts for our lives. When we're awake, we act out the scenes. So I view every moment as an important event in life. Everything we experience has a higher purpose, a deeper meaning.

We can gain insight into this by asking ourselves questions and trying to understand the meaning behind the events in our lives. What lesson am I supposed to learn from this experience? What lesson am I teaching? How will this experience make me grow?

Nothing in life is meaningless. Even the negative things in life have their place. The frustrations we sometimes feel are there for a reason. Usually the most frustrating events in our lives are the best indication of the lessons we are supposed to be learning.

The violence and loss we sometimes encounter have a higher meaning. I don't presume to know all the answers, but I still believe it all has a purpose.

Self-identity: You are not your body

When you are out of your body, you are a ghost or a spirit. When this hits home, you realize that we're all just spirits, temporarily inhabiting physical bodies. You no longer think of yourself as just the physical body. Your physical body is just an expression of your true self, your soul. You recognize that the needs and desires of your physical body are different from the needs and desires of your soul. Your body is just a tool you are using. Instead of thinking in terms of statements like "I am hungry," you start to think in terms of "My body is hungry." You are no longer a slave to the physical body and its whims. You can brush aside the complaints of your body with a "get over it" attitude.

Likewise, everyone else is also a spirit, so it doesn't make sense to judge people by the color of their skin, their gender, their weight, their looks, or any other physical attributes. Spirit transcends all of these boundaries. You also realize that if you hurt another person, you are hurting yourself.

A greater reality

Every day most of us get up early in the morning, go to work, come home tired, eat, watch television, then go to bed. Sometimes, we interact with people. Throughout our mundane existence, we walk around with blinders on, seeing what we want to see and believing what we want to believe. We see ourselves as trapped inside a physical body, and we measure our own success by the physical possessions we own. Most of the time, we fail to recognize the spiritual world that surrounds us.

There is only one reality, not many, but it's a multidimensional spiritual reality with many worlds. We are surrounded by spirits and angels. Every cell and every object is permeated with the light of God's being. If you take a deeper look, it seems as if our "reality" is no more than a daydream held in God's imagination.

We're never alone

Out-of-body experiences have taught me that we are never alone. Even when I am alone in my bedroom, when I leave my body, I may be surrounded by spirits and helpers.

Privacy is an illusion

Because we are never alone, and these spirits can read our thoughts, there is no such thing as privacy. Privacy is an illusion. I've had many OBEs in which I found myself in someone's home, witnessing their private lives. There are no secrets in the spirit world. Once you realize that, you learn to live your life with more pure and spiritual thoughts.

Don't judge others

After a few OBEs, you start to realize that most other people are operating from a very limited physical-body point of view, and they don't have the perspective you have. You realize that from our limited physical-body point of view, we simply don't have enough information to make judgments about other people. You don't know their belief systems, motivations, or the lessons they are learning. You learn not to judge other people. This isn't anything new; Christ taught it two thousand years ago.

Physical objects lose their glitter

When we use out-of-body experiences to take a look behind the scenes of life, we start to view physical objects as transient. We begin to see that physical objects are only temporary, and sooner or later we have to give them all up. The only thing we take from this lifetime is our experiences.

When we own a physical object, we should keep future owners in mind. I'm a woodworker. When I make something out of wood, I know that it has a limited lifetime. I see physical objects as shallow and unimportant, so I try to give the object a deeper meaning. For example, I once made a box for knickknacks and I gave it a spiritual value as well as a physical value by engraving the following motto on it:

Focus:
Will ....To accomplish your dreams
Heart...........Because love conquers all
Mind ....The answers are within
Soul ....The real you lies beyond your body

When we own physical objects, we are borrowing them from Mother Earth. My wife and I love to travel, and I've been to a lot of archeological sites to see the remains of ancient civilizations: ancient cities in Egypt, Italy, Greece, and ancient Mayan cities like Tikal. It's amazing to see how a thousand years can crumble the mightiest civilizations into dust. Mankind has labored for thousands of years to build physical objects, but they're all just temporary, and therefore not as important as the things we keep inside: our thoughts, feelings, lessons, joys, and loves.

Most people are familiar with a saying that's so materialistic it's funny: "He who dies with the most toys wins." There are people who believe this. I'd rather spend money traveling, meeting people, and learning lessons than buying physical things.

Death is an illusion

When you're out of your body, you can visit dead relatives. In my first book, I wrote about an OBE where I met and spoke with my dad after his death. Since that time, my perspective on death has changed. I know that my dad is still very much "alive" in the astral world, because I met him there. I know that when he died, he left his body behind for good, and that his physical body is no longer a part of his life.

Every Memorial Day, my mother goes to the gravesites of dead relatives. She goes there to remember the dead, and maybe to pray. I never go with her to visit graves, and because of that, she probably thinks that I'm uncaring, unfeeling, or maybe not sentimental. One time she asked me if I ever go to visit my dad's gravesite. "No," I told her. I don't need to visit the site of his dead physical body for several reasons.

First, he's not using it anymore. He doesn't have any sentimental attachment to that body anymore. The act of visiting his dead body probably doesn't hold any special significance to him; besides, I'd much rather visit *him* than his grave. Second, I don't need to be at his gravesite to remember him, think about him, or pray for him. I know in my heart that anytime I need or want my dad, he will come to my side. Sometimes I feel his presence by my side when I'm not even thinking about him. "Hi, Dad." I try to tell him in my mind, "How's it going? What else have you learned over there?" Maybe it's my imagination, but I even seem to receive a reply in my head, "I learned that there's a lot more to life on your side than I ever imagined when I was there." Isn't every day Memorial Day?

Death is a friend

Death is a friend because it teaches us that every day is precious. We are only given a limited number of days, so we should use them wisely. My brother Tom once said, "Every day above ground is a good day."

I'm not afraid to die because I've seen that my consciousness is not dependent on my physical body. Every time I have an OBE I am reminded that my time is running out, and eventually I'll have to leave that body for good.

Many people who have near-death experiences experience a "life review," where they relive their entire life. During the review, they find themselves thinking about the consequences of their actions and how other people felt toward them. I try to view everything from the perspective of an end-of-life review. How are my actions affecting other people? What am I learning from this experience? Am I making someone's life a little bit brighter or darker? How will this look on my spiritual scorecard?

My dad had many stories locked inside his head, about hunting and fishing trips and his time in the Air Force. He always talked about publishing his stories in a book. He even had a name for his book: *Sojourn*, a word that means a temporary stay. When he died, I expected to find a half-written book, or a box full of notes and stories. Instead, I found nothing but a title page. He never wrote any of his stories, so the book was never published. He had an opportunity to give the world a message, tell some stories, make someone happy for years after his death, but he never did. We all have that opportunity. What will *you* do with your opportunity?

Often I ask myself, "When I die, what will I leave for this world?" Something worthwhile, I hope. Since you don't know when you'll die, when is the best time to accomplish your dreams? Now.

Why do we spend thousands of dollars to bury someone's physical body in a fancy box with a beautiful wood finish and plush interior? Once you're dead, you won't be needing that body anymore, and you won't be using that fancy box it's in. As far as I'm concerned, it's a huge waste of time and money. I don't care what they do with my body when I die because I won't be using it anymore. I'd rather see my body put to some productive use: Donate the whole thing to science! Don't try to keep it from decomposing. Return my body to the food chain where it belongs. Leave it in the woods so some bear or wolf can have a feast, or throw it into the ocean and feed it to the fish. I'd rather give my body back to nature. In Tibet, it's customary to set dead bodies out in the sun so that vultures can eat them. They call it a sky burial.

What if people misunderstand me?

People are always questioning my motives for sharing my experiences. They ask me, "Is it true? Are these experiences real or are you just a fiction writer?" I assure you that my experiences are real and that my writing about them has been to help other people understand and explore. I don't want money. I don't want fame. My writing is meant to give people new hope for spirituality in this universe, because I have experienced it directly and wish others could too. It is meant to ease the pain of losing someone close who has died, because I have seen them myself and so can you. It is meant to inspire hope that there is an afterlife, because I have been there myself, and so can you.

I hope that my writings give hope to those who need it. Maybe it can help someone discover their higher purpose, or find a way out of depression. I mentioned that we have all chosen to come to this Earth for a spiritual purpose. We must all learn to rise above our earthly ruts and glitches because they are so petty when compared to the world of the spirit. If I can inspire that hope and spirituality in only one person, it will all have been worth it.

Conclusions

Bridging the gap between science and the supernatural has always been one of my dreams. Since my childhood, my heroes have been people who have tried to bridge that gap, like Leonardo da Vinci, Robert Monroe, Charles Tart, and Otto Schmitt. I've always felt that if science and the supernatural can be reconciled, many of the illusions that we live with (such as separation from loved ones when they die, and various religious superstitions) will be eliminated. When science can seriously explore and establish facts on issues such as (1) the nature of psychic experiences; (2) the nature of the afterlife, the soul, and spirits; and (3) the nature of God, then perhaps we can agree on "what to believe" and do away with all the fighting over religious differences. Maybe we can all agree that we are spiritual beings first and foremost, and we should all work toward spiritual growth. Maybe we can also learn to set aside our materialism for pursuits that are more spiritual. And if science can't establish these things as facts, at least OBEs can help each of us learn these things at a personal level.

PART TWO

TWENTY YEARS OF OUT-OF-BODY RESEARCH

18

EXPLORE YOUR WORLD
. . . AND OTHERS!

There is no love greater than God's love,
And there is no purpose greater than
God's love shining through us.

—Inner Voice

What is the purpose of space exploration? What does it gain us? Most scientists would argue that the value of space exploration is that it tells us about the universe and its origins, and that brings us a greater understanding of humanity and our place in the universe.

In 1997, just a few weeks prior to the release of my first book, NASA landed the Pathfinder robot on the surface of Mars, where it began taking pictures and soil samples. At the time, it was the biggest event the Internet had ever seen, as hundreds of millions of people across the world were enthralled at the photographs taken from the surface of the strange and alien world called Mars. Even so, *every one* of those people had the ability to actually set foot in a strange, if different, new world—one that has been called "the astral plane."

Every day, thousands of people stand on the brink of that new world—the world beyond—then, eventually, they fall in, shedding their physical body in an act we call death. They tragically go into that world ignorant, uninformed, and inexperienced, but information about it is readily available through OBEs. It's not hard to find instructions on how to get there, so why aren't people doing it?

The Discovery Channel's motto is "Explore your world." My motto is "Why limit yourself to just one world?"

Throughout the Mars Pathfinder event, I thought to myself, "Wake up, guys! Every one of you has the ability, not only to see the landscape of a different world, but also to actually go there. Mars? No problemo! But why stop there? You have nine planets to choose from in this solar system alone. Beyond that, billions and billions of stars with planets circling around them." Now that Carl Sagan has passed on, I can just imagine his delight at exploring the "billions and billions" of stars that he loved to dream about while he was alive.

Why stop there? Beyond our physical world lie other worlds, nonphysical worlds, worlds of untold wonder and beauty that are patiently waiting for our arrival. We don't need any special equipment or space vehicles to get there. We don't need any special breathing apparatus to survive there. There are no vast distances to be crossed to get there.

How can our government spend billions of dollars and decades of research to land a robot on a distant planet, but not invest the time and patience required to explore the out-of-body worlds? The "costs" associated with OBE exploration are negligible:

Time: Learning the skill can take time.

Patience: Because it's so hard to describe, learning how to achieve OBE states can involve some trial and error. Like any skill, patience is required.

Belief: Actually, belief is not a requirement. When I had my first OBE, I was skeptical. Perhaps it's more appropriate to say that suspension of disbelief is required. Many new-age thinkers insist that our experiences are governed by our beliefs.

Advantages of the OBE over Space Exploration

• Space exploration will *never* tell us what lies beyond the veil of death.

• OBE costs less.

• No special equipment is needed for OBEs.

• No special education or degrees are required for OBEs.

• I believe space exploration is limited by space-time. I believe OBEs are not.

• Since we are spiritual beings, space exploration will never have as much spiritual impact as exploration of the nonphysical world through OBEs.

- OBEs can tell us *more* about ourselves and our place in the universe.

OBE Disadvantages

It wouldn't be fair if I mentioned all the advantages of OBE without mentioning some of the disadvantages.

- With OBEs, you can't collect any physical samples. You can't record any data.

- You may have to give up some limiting beliefs.

- You may have to face some fears, such as fear of the unknown and fear of death, but let's face it, the Apollo astronauts also had to face their fears of dying.

Humankind has been "accidentally" bumping into the nonphysical universe for countless centuries, so OBE explorations are certainly nothing new. Shamans from all around the world have one thing in common: the claim that they can leave their body.

The twentieth century saw exponential advances in technology. Today's palm-top computers are thousands of times more powerful than the massive mainframes that guided the Apollo missions to the Moon, and that was just twenty-five years ago. Fifty years ago, a single computer would fill a large room and still not have the computing power of the hand-held calculators of twenty-five years ago. Despite the technological advances we've made, our spiritual progress has not been exponential. Perhaps today we're more "politically correct" and "sensitive" to the needs of others. That's a good start, but there's a lot more to spirituality than treating each other with respect. Early last century, in the 1920s, there were a few brave individuals who started to explore out-of-body experiences seriously by inducing them. People like Sylvan Muldoon, Hugh Calloway (a.k.a. Oliver Fox), and Edward Peach (a.k.a. Ophiel) led the way. Fifty years later, in the 1970s, Robert Monroe joined the ranks and began his own journeys. But the exploration has been far from matching the exponential growth of the computer industry.

How can anyone not be excited about the opportunities for exploration?

19

THE CONTINUUM OF CONSCIOUSNESS: DISTINGUISHING OBEs FROM OTHER PHENOMENA

*I was feeling particularly religious, and thought
    to myself, "God, I am your servant."
My inner voice stepped up and said,
"No. You are God's will, not God's servant.
You are not a serf, but rather an emissary.
    Everyone is."*

One thing I've learned through the years is that we are not as closely tied to our bodies as we might think. Most people who believe in astral projection think that we have multiple bodies, such as the astral body, the etheric body that can exit our physical body. That belief probably comes from experience; when people have OBEs, they usually have a body image that's deeply ingrained in them while they're awake. We're accustomed to getting sensory input in the shape of our physical body.

I don't think we need an astral "body" at all; it's just a basic part of our belief system. Change that part of your belief system and your awareness may take the form of a ball of energy, a sphere of awareness, or a pin-point of consciousness.

Many people view death as some huge chasm or gulf that needs to be crossed. Once dead, we get to the proverbial Other Side. Even most astral travelers believe in the "astral plane," a place that is separate from our ordinary existence. I don't like to think of the astral plane as a separate place. I prefer to think that we are always surrounded and engulfed by many places that all boil down to one thing: dimensions of being. We live in these dimensions all the time, but most of the time we're so focused on our physical senses that we block out the information from those other places. But that doesn't make them separate from where we are now.

Radio stations seem separate from each other because of the technology we use to transmit and receive. In reality, they are all using tiny portions of the same unified electromagnetic spectrum to broadcast signals. I believe that there is a similar unified spectrum of consciousness on which we are constantly existing and interacting. For example, your conscious mind may be communicating with the conscious mind of another person, through physical mediums like sound waves (speaking and listening) or through light waves (sign language); at the same time, your subconscious mind may be sending and receiving telepathic information from another person at the astral level.[16]

---

[16] Whenever I try to talk to an in-the-body person during an OBE, I seem to be talking to their subconscious mind. They typically have no conscious memory of the conversation. See chapter 21 of my book *Out of Body Experiences* for more information.

At the same time, our higher self may be interacting with the higher self of yet another person who exists at a level higher than the astral plane.

Consciousness extends well beyond the realm of OBEs. You and I are "ghosts," born and raised on a higher plane, temporarily visiting this sphere of existence. Or as rock musician Sting would sing, "We are spirits in the material world." The main difference between other spirits and us is some excess baggage: physical bodies. We are all "astrally challenged" ghosts. We cut ourselves off from our native environment, the nonphysical worlds. So what holds us "inside" our bodies? Only our beliefs. Once you get beyond that, you allow your consciousness to "blur" into other levels of existence. You start to experience phenomena like out-of-body experiences.

There are many phenomena similar to OBEs that show us how unconstrained our consciousness really is. Sometimes, when we think strongly about a close friend, a portion of our consciousness is transported there while we are still inside the body. Some of these "visits" can be unintentional. People routinely visit each other in their dreams and may or may not remember it.

To complicate matters, experiences of other worlds don't always translate well into physical words, so we find confusing terms in mystical and occult literature. One of the most common questions I receive goes something like this: "The other day this happened. . . . Was it an OBE?" To try to clear up some of the confusion, I'd like to propose some definitions. These definitions are not meant to be clinical definitions, they are meant for the layperson.

Out-of-Body Experience (OBE)

An out-of-body experience is an experience in which your entire consciousness (100%) seems to be separated (apart) from your physical body. During an OBE, your physical body is just another inanimate object in the room, and it contains virtually no sense of conscious awareness. OBEs are fully conscious experiences. Some people may disagree with this definition, but for now let's define it this way and I'll discuss the conflicts in definition later.

Astral Projection

Occultists, Theosophists, and Spiritualists started using the term astral projection in the late 1800s and early 1900s to refer to out-of-body experiences. Since that time, the term has been used to mean a variety of things. Some people say that astral projection is different from out-of-body experiences because you are visiting a different place, the astral plane, not just walking around your bedroom or somewhere else in the physical location. I don't think the distinction is important, so I define astral projection as an out-of-body experience. They're the same thing.

Hypnagogic/Hypnopompic Imagery

The hypnagogic state is the natural state of drowsiness preceding sleep. There is a similar state of consciousness before we're fully awake, known as the hypnopompic state. It's quite normal to see vivid (often moving) images (hallucinations) and hear vivid voices during the hypnagogic and hypnopompic states.

I haven't heard of people reporting hypnagogic touches, smells, or tastes; usually they report voices or faces. This is a normal, natural phenomenon that occurs to everyone as they get closer to sleep or awakening.

While working to induce my out-of-body experiences, I've learned how to induce this state quickly and with full awareness. I sometimes amuse myself watching and listening to the hypnagogic imagery. Usually it doesn't make any sense at all; I see pictures of people I don't know, and hear fragments of sentences, or sometimes full sentences. For me, it's always been in English. There's nothing systematic or organized about this imagery as far as I can tell.

Near-Death Experience (NDE)

This is an experience in which the subject becomes very nearly dead. Typically, they have an out-of-body experience as part of their NDE. Unlike OBEs, NDEs typically have other features that are not normally found in classic OBEs. One example is the panoramic life review common to the NDE. People who have an NDE often report seeing their lives flash before their eyes and claim that they literally experience their *entire* lifetime over again, as if watching it on television. This doesn't normally happen during a typical OBE.

Robert Monroe's Focus Level Experiences

In his book *Journeys Out of the Body*, Robert Monroe clearly described out-of-body experiences. His OBEs led him to start exploring other altered states of consciousness. As he progressed, he put labels on the different states of consciousness. He called them "focus levels." For example, he defined Focus 10 (or F-10) as "Body asleep, mind awake." He developed a world-renowned organization (The Monroe Institute in Faber, Virginia) dedicated to teaching people how to reach various focus levels and states of consciousness. He also wrote about his focus level experiences in two more books: *Far Journeys* (Doubleday 1985) and *Ultimate Journey* (Doubleday 1994).

I believe many people mistake these "focus level experiences" for out-of-body experiences. Monroe Institute voyagers like Rosalind McKnight (1999) label their experiences OBEs. Since I did not join her in her journeys, I cannot say how much of McKnight's consciousness was "outside" and how much was "inside" her body, but I assume that some portion of her consciousness remained inside her body because the majority of her experiences were narrated, which I believe would be impossible for someone whose entire consciousness was out of the body. Therefore, with less than 100% consciousness, her experiences do not fit my definition of an OBE.

Other people adept in Monroe's techniques, such as Bruce Moen, have made it clear they are *not* out-of-body experiences, at least not by my definition. Most, if not all of these "focus level experiences" take place while a good portion of consciousness is still located inside the traveler's body.

That's not to say that focus level experiences are less valid or "real" than OBEs. On the contrary, authors like Moen, in his books *Voyages into the Unknown* and *Voyage beyond Doubt* (1997 and 1999), have presented remarkable evidence that their minds can meet and interact with other voyagers on the same focus level, in the same objective (not subjective) realm of existence. That's a feat that has yet to be done with OBEs.

Robert Monroe described a continuum of consciousness, alluding to the fact that we all have the ability to send *varying amounts* of our conscious awareness to locations outside the body. This is affirmed by other Monroe followers such as Patricia Leva in *Traveling the Interstate of Consciousness: A Driver's Instruction Manual* (1998). Some authors have suggested that we call focus level experiences "Type 2 OBEs," whereas "Type 1 OBEs" fit my definition above. Based on my experience of both OBEs and Monroe journeys, it makes more sense to define an OBE as a separate phenomenon. In honor of the late Monroe who inspired my OBE exploration, I'd like to call these "Monroe focus level experiences."

Soul Traveling

This is a term coined by the Eckankar religion to denote out-of-body travel. According to Eckankar, soul travel is "the ability of Soul to transcend the physical body and travel into the spiritual worlds of God." Other authors have used this term to denote out-of-body travel. Some authors like Albert Taylor and Dr. Bruce Goldberg write about OBEs, but call it soul travel. Perhaps the term soul travel should be reserved for Eckankar's use to avoid confusion.

Dream Visits

A dream visit is when a person travels to another location "in a dream." Some of these dreams can be remarkable in their accuracy, leading us to conclude that something is leaving the body and traveling to a remote location (see *Dreamgates* by Robert Moss, 1998). Once again, what distinguishes this phenomenon from OBE is the fact that full consciousness is not present. The dreamer recognizes the experience as an unconscious (or maybe conscious) dream experience, rather than an OBE. Again, I don't mean to imply that these experiences are any less valid than OBEs. In chapter 25, I address the differences between OBEs, dreams, and lucid dreams.

Remote Viewing

Here psychics can send their minds to a remote location to "see" what's there. Unlike OBEs, remote viewing takes place with your consciousness firmly rooted *inside* your body. You're just "seeing" images of things that are happening elsewhere.

Traveling Clairvoyance

This term was commonly used during the height of the Spiritualist movement in the late 1800s and early 1900s. Mediums and psychics were asked to mentally visit a remote location, sometimes under hypnosis. Again, the majority of the subject's consciousness was located inside the body. This is probably equivalent to remote viewing.

Almost-There Experiences

When I documented OBEs in my journals, they were always full-blown, fully conscious, no-doubt-about-it genuine OBEs. Anything less I did not consider an OBE.

In late 1980, I began to experience another strange phenomenon that I called the "almost-there experience." The ATE was just like an OBE, but I wasn't fully conscious. Sometimes I could remember episodes that were just barely out of conscious reach.

For example, one time when I woke up, I remembered being on the astral plane, talking with friends. I remembered saying, "Well, I've got to go now." The astral friend said, "Are you sure you're going to remember this experience?" Confidently, I said, "Sure. I'll remember." Then I woke up. I knew I had an experience similar to an OBE, but my consciousness wasn't 100% clear, so I didn't call it an OBE.

The important point here is that we should strive to gain more consciousness and memory of what happens during our sleep time. Although most dreams are just plays that we enact to work out problems, there is more to sleep than dreaming. Some people claim that we can learn to become completely conscious during our entire sleep experience, remembering all the stages of sleep. If that is true, we might not have to feel like a third of our lives is wasted time.

Bilocation

Bilocation is more common to mystics, saints, and holy people. This is the experience of being *physically* located in two or more places at the same time. The subject may be seen, heard, touched, etc. To the eyewitness, it seems as if that person is actually there physically, not in some sort of ghostly body, as in an OBE.

Scrying

Scrying is the deliberate act of perceiving events that lie beyond the range of the physical senses by using the agents of the unconscious mind (Tyson 1997, p. 3). In that regard, it is much more akin to controlled remote viewing than it is OBE. An object (like a crystal ball) is normally used in scrying, whereas remote viewing doesn't require one.

Sleep Paralysis/False Awakening

Sleep paralysis is a normal, natural thing your body does every night. The physical body needs to be paralyzed during sleep so that we don't act out our dreams (e.g., thrashing our arms and legs, sleepwalking, etc.). Sometimes people become conscious while their body is still paralyzed for sleep.

When this happens to me, I find myself out of my body, but unable to move astrally or physically. It is possible to free yourself from your body during sleep paralysis, but for me it's been very difficult. It's almost easier to induce an OBE from a waking state than from sleep paralysis.

When people have conscious experiences of sleep paralysis, it's called "false awakening" because it may seem like they wake up, but their body remains asleep for a short period of time. These experiences are often very frightening to people who don't understand what's happening. Often, they frantically try to get back inside their body or "wake up" but nothing seems to work. Sometimes it seems as if they wake up, but after a few minutes, they realize they're still asleep and dreaming, so they try to "wake up" again. Sometimes the cycle of false awakenings repeats itself several times.

Since fears can manifest into reality in this state, people often report seeing creatures or old hags who try to attack them or sit on them. These attacks have also been called "hagging" experiences. Once a person understands what's happening, he can stop being afraid, which leads to more positive experiences.

Autoscopy

This is a clinical syndrome where you see an image of yourself, like the classical Doppelgänger. When it happens, your consciousness remains in the body, and you see an image or phantom of yourself. Occultists say you are seeing your astral body in this experience.

Depersonalization

A person experiencing depersonalization does not necessarily feel "out of body." Rather, they experience a split between the observing self and the functioning self. Accident victims sometimes report that they experienced the event as if it were happening to someone else. There are several variations, such as feeling that your body is dead or numb, feeling detached from your self-image, or having the sense that you are watching yourself from a distance.

Schizophrenia

Some people have compared OBEs with schizophrenic body boundary disturbances, but they are two very different things.

In the 1980s, two psychiatrists, Glen Gabbard and Stuart Twemlow, analyzed the OBE from a psychological perspective. They published their findings in *With the Eyes of the Mind: An Empirical Analysis of Out-of-Body States* (1984). Anyone who is interested in studying the psychology of OBEs should read it. Each chapter compares the OBE with another psychological phenomenon. According to Gabbard and Twemlow, schizophrenics have a loss of reality testing,[17] often accompanied by psychosis, paranoia and hallucinations, but people who have OBEs have no problems with reality testing and tend to be free from mental illness (1984, p. 89). Schizophrenics may not know where their bodies are, but people having OBEs know where their *bodies* are, just not where *they* are!

---

[17]Reality testing refers to a person's ability to discern, perceive, appreciate, or "test" the qualities of their surroundings.

20

OBEs AND ORGANIZED RELIGION

"What's today's lesson?" I asked my inner voice.
"You imagine God is outside of you, and so God is.
Today, I want you to imagine that God is right
    there inside you.
Watching your every move, guiding your every
    footstep,
sharing your laughs, your dreams and your goals."

You don't need to be religious to have an out-of-body experience,[18] but OBEs often change a person's outlook to be more religious.[19]

People often ask me if astral projection is breaking some kind of cosmic law. They are afraid that God

---

[18]In *Flight of Mind: A Psychological Study of the Out-of-Body Experience*, H. J. Irwin states, "In short, there is no conclusive evidence that (intellectually) religious variables contribute to either the occurrence or the content of the OBE" (1985, p. 189).

[19]Again, I quote *Flight of Mind:* "For example, Ring (1980, pp. 160–161) reports enhanced religiosity among people, particularly women, who had an OBE or at least an NDE in life-threatening circumstances" (Irwin 1985, p. 216).

might be unhappy with them, and so they want assur-
ance from me that it is all right. While I won't pretend
to know how God feels about this, I have spent some
time studying how some of the different religions see
astral travel.

There is no doubt that all of the great religions of
the world are based upon the religious experiences of
their founders. In some cases these experiences may
have been OBEs. There are references to OBEs in
many of the holy texts of the world's major religions.

Christianity

Enoch—The man who walked with God

There are passages in the Bible that I believe
directly relate to OBEs. Genesis 5:21–24 talks about
Enoch, the great-great-great grandfather of Noah. It
mentions that Enoch "walked with God for three hun-
dred and sixty-five years" and eventually Enoch was
not seen again because "God had taken him away." In
Jude 1:14, it references the Book of Enoch, which is a
biblical text removed from the Bible by early Catholic
Church authorities because it was considered too con-
troversial for common people. For some people, it may
seem unreasonable to accept that the Bible has been
edited by men of authority, but in fact it is true. The
original Bible was copied several times and brought to
then distant places like Ethiopia before it was edited by
the Catholic Church. A few of these early Bibles still
remain, and they still contain the original texts like the
Book of Enoch. There were also fragments of the Book
of Enoch found among the Dead Sea Scrolls.

The Book of Enoch is mostly about Enoch, and
what he saw when he "walked with God" as described

in Genesis. The entire Book of Enoch text can be found in books such as *The Old Testament Pseude-pigrapha* (Charlesworth 1983). The text describes classical OBE symptoms: "And in the vision, the winds were causing me to fly and rushing me high up into heaven. And I kept coming into heaven until I approached a wall which was built of white marble and surrounded by tongues of fire; and it frightened me . . . fear covered me and trembling seized me" (1 Enoch 14:8–14).

The Prophet Elisha

The second book of Kings describes a time when the Israelites were at war with Aram. The prophet Elisha kept the Jews out of danger by using what many believe is astral projection to see the battle plans of their enemy: "Elisha, the prophet in Israel, . . . tells the king of Israel the very words that you speak in your bedchamber" (2 Kings 6:8–14).

The Apostle Paul

Some people believe that the Apostle Paul was able to astrally project. In his first letter to the Corinthians, Paul says that he "dies" every day. Maybe he meant that he leaves his body every day: "Every day I die: I swear it by my pride in you . . ." (1 Corinthians 15:31).

Later, Paul goes on to talk about the astral body: "As we have worn the likeness of the man made of dust, so we shall wear the likeness of the heavenly man" (1 Corinthians 15:49).

In his second letter to the Corinthians, Paul talks about a Christian man who may have had OBEs: "I know a Christian man who fourteen years ago (whether in the body or out of it, I do not know—God knows) was caught up as far as the third heaven. And I know that this same man (whether in the body or out of it, I do not know—God knows) was caught up into paradise, and heard words so secret that human lips may not repeat them" (2 Corinthians 12:2–4).

This—in Paul's own words—affirms that it's okay for Christians to use out-of-body experiences to gain direct knowledge of God. Some people believe that Paul was writing about his own personal experiences, but attributed them to someone else due to his modesty.

The Book of Revelation

I also believe that the Revelation of John (the Book of Revelation) was one long out-of-body experience: "After this I looked up, and there before my eyes was a door opened in heaven; and the voice that I had first heard speaking to me like a trumpet said, 'Come up here, and I will show you what must happen hereafter.' At once I was caught up by the Spirit. There in heaven stood a throne . . . " (Revelation 4:1–2).

I think that, if asked, most Christians would discourage the practice of astral projection. Perhaps they are afraid that you will learn your own truths instead of following what they want you to believe. What they don't know is this: with astral projection, you can directly experience God. If you want, you can meet Jesus Christ in person. Instead of saying that you have a relationship with God, learn astral projection, and you can *really* experience God. Instead of praying to Jesus Christ, meet the man. Look into his eyes, embrace him, and talk with him in person.

Islam

Islamic traditions say that the prophet Muhammad ascended to heaven and was shown the tortures of hell and the joys of paradise. The Qur'an sura 17, called *Surat al-isra* (The Night Journey, Children of Israel) speaks of a nightly journey that might be an OBE: "Glory to (Allah) Who did take His servant for a Journey by night from the Sacred Mosque to the farthest Mosque, whose precincts We did bless, in order that We might show him some of Our Signs: for He is the One Who heareth and seeth (all things)" (Ali 1987).

Buddhism

Buddhism also has a tradition of out-of-body travel. I.P. Couliano notes: "The art of leaving the body was also known to Buddhist monks, who explored the western paradise of *Amitābha* even before going there to abide after death. This seems to be a shamanistic interpretation of Buddhist *dhyana* (meditation) in terms of an otherworldly journey" (Couliano 1991, p. 76).

The most famous work regarding the afterlife, the *Bardo Thodol,* or The Tibetan Book of the Dead, was most likely based on out-of-body observations.

Hinduism

Out-of-body experiences are also referenced in the Hindu religion. Books like *Easy Journey to Other Planets* by A. C. Bhaktivedanta Swami Prabhupada go into great detail regarding transcendence of the material world and entry into the "anti-material world": "Those who have realized the transcendence can reach the anti-material world by leaving their material bodies during the period of *uttarayana,* that is, when the sun is on its northern path, or during auspicious moments in which the deities of fire and effulgence control the atmosphere" (1970, p. 20).

Another important Hindu text, The Upanishads, talks about other-worldly journeys, saying that a person should not be awakened suddenly because the soul might be in danger of not finding its way back to the body.[20]

In Paramahansa Yogananda's translation/interpretation of the Bhagavad Gita, he wrote that the ideal person, who has the power of continuous contact with God, will be adept in astral projection. "His perception will be through intuition; interplanetary and interastral travel will be accomplished not by airplanes or atomic airships, but by instantaneous astral projection" (Yogananda 1995, p. 736).

Shamanism

Shamanism is the native religion of many indigenous peoples all over the globe. Various forms of this religion can be found in North America (Native Americans), South America, China, Russia, Africa, and everywhere else in the world.

Every organized religion has living people who interact with God and the afterlife. In Christianity this

---

[20]According to Couliano, this is in the Brhadaranyaka Upanishad 4.3.14 (Couliano 1991, p. 88).

role is assumed by priests, ministers, and so on. In Judaism, it is assumed by rabbis. The central figure in shamanism is the shaman, or medicine man. The religious practices and beliefs of shamans vary from culture to culture, but they all have one thing in common: the shaman can induce out-of-body experiences. The shaman travels out of body to heal, prophesy, find missing people, and perform other functions.

Witches' Sabbat

The practice of witchcraft was originally based upon pagan old-world religions before they were suppressed by Christianity. Much of the practice was passed on by word of mouth. Sometime around the fourteenth century, people started talking about women who "flew" to attend a gathering known as the Sabbat. I believe these nocturnal rides were out-of-body experiences, and much of the beliefs were probably passed down from ancient practices of earlier European shamans. The "old religion," as it was called, had nothing to do with Satan or Satanism. The Catholic Church held an effective smear campaign that changed the public's image of witchcraft to be associated with evil. The first known images of a witch riding a broom appeared in the year 1280. Today, some people practice a more modern form of this religion, called Wicca, which still teaches astral projection.

Other Out-of-Body Folklore

Much of the world's folklore can also be attributed to out-of-body experiences. Tales of vampires, were-wolves, and other forms of shape-shifting probably evolved from OBEs in which the astral body takes on nonhuman form. Some of these undoubtedly stem from drug-induced experiences of shamans, but I believe much of it came from natural nightly excursions. That's why tales of shape-shifting usually portray the transformation occurring at night.

Clearly, out-of-body experiences have had a major impact on the world's religions. The fact that OBEs appear in the texts of the major world religions tells me that there aren't conflicts between OBE and religion. Ultimately, people must decide for themselves how OBEs fit into their belief system. We all have the power to induce OBEs and find our own answers.

21

THE PROBLEM OF
OBTAINING PROOF

"What is love?" I asked my inner voice.
"Love is the hitching post of the universe."
—Inner Voice

People sometimes ask me to "prove" to them that my out-of-body experiences are "real," and not merely flights of the imagination. What people don't seem to understand is that proof is an elusive thing, even in our physical world. Suppose someone named John sends me an e-mail asking me to "prove" that my experiences are real by visiting him in his home and reporting what I see on his desk. Let's take a look at how I might approach such a task and some of the problems involved.

Problem 1. I don't know where John lives.

My first problem is that I don't know where John lives. He could be anywhere in the world for all I know. Let's assume that John gives me a precise address: 315 East Baker Street, Cleveland, Ohio, USA.

Problem 2. How do I get to Cleveland?

I could try several approaches to get to Cleveland, but some methods work better than others. Walking doesn't work well because it would take me weeks to walk from Minneapolis to Cleveland under the best conditions. Closing my eyes and trying to "will" myself to Cleveland might work (I'll discuss this later), but it isn't always reliable. I could fall into the fantasy trap, which essentially leads me into the lucid dreaming state where I'm dreaming/hallucinating a subconscious version of John's house. If I managed to avoid the fantasy trap, I might just as easily black out and find myself back inside my body, especially if I get at all excited at the prospect of obtaining proof. I have an equal chance of going nowhere. So let's assume for now that I choose to "fly" to John's house.

Problem 3. How do I find Cleveland?

My first step is to soar through the air, but in what direction do I go? Let's assume that I know Cleveland is about 760 miles southeast of Minneapolis by car. The problem is, I have no radios, no navigation equipment, no compass. I'm not a pilot, so I can't recognize landmarks from the air. As soon as I'm out of the city of Minneapolis, the scenery is unfamiliar to me. The patches of farmland start to look the same from the air, especially if it's dark out (it's not uncommon to have OBEs at night), winter (snow on the fields), cloudy weather (if you're flying above the clouds), or I'm at a high altitude from which the landmarks are too tiny to tell much. Let's assume that all these problems are overcome, and somehow I make it to Cleveland.

Problem 4. How do I find John's street in Cleveland?

Even if I could make it to Cleveland, I would arrive there without any maps, nor any sense of direction. I don't know any of the street names. Even if I knew the name of John's street, where is it in relation to the rest of the city? For that matter, where did I land in relation to the rest of the city? Let's assume for a moment that I studied a map of Cleveland before I left, and memorized the street names. I still don't know any of the land-marks. Regardless of that, I could look at a street sign, immediately identify where I was, and determine the correct direction to walk or fly to get to John's house.

Problem 5. How do I find John's house?

Even if I could find the street, it might take me a long time to find the right house. How could I distin-guish John's house from every other house on the same street? Let's assume all I have is the street address. Suppose I walk down the street looking at the house numbers until I find the right house.

Problem 6. How do I find the desk inside the house?

Once inside the house, the next challenge would be finding the desk. I could systematically try every room in the house until I came across one with a desk, but that takes time, and time is a scarce commodity during an OBE (although OBEs can last longer than an hour, most last only a few minutes).

What I'd like is a way to shortcut the process and avoid all the searching and guesswork. There are two possibilities: to ask for guidance from astral helpers, or trust in some kind of cosmic guidance to find it. Both are hit-and-miss, but I've used them both with some measure of success. Sometimes I'll get there and sometimes I'll be whisked away to some totally unexpected place.

The solution is to simplify the problem. Devise a controlled laboratory experiment where the physical distance is minimized. Put the target in a locked room next to where the subject is lying. There have been a few similar experiments where objective reality has apparently been viewed during an OBE and later verified. For example, Robert Monroe and "Miss Z" were studied by Charles Tart, and they performed some amazing OBE feats, such as reading off a random five-digit number that was hidden.[21]

Problem 7. There are differences between astral and physical reality.

Astral reality can be confusing for several reasons. First, we don't know the rules because we're not used to being there. Second, we're so accustomed to using our physical senses that astral senses may seem foreign and unfamiliar. In my first book, I described three different types of astral sight: astral sight, astral mind sensing, and clairvoyant sight. Third, our physical brain isn't used to translating astral experiences into physical terms. For example, if you "look" at something during an OBE, you might be "seeing" it from all angles at once (astral mind sensing), but your brain tries to translate that experience into terms it knows, as

---

[21]Susan Blackmore covers this topic well in chapter 18 of the 1992 edition of *Beyond the Body: An Investigation of Out-of-the-Body Experiences*.

images imprinted on the retina. Its interpretation isn't always accurate or easy to describe.

Problem 8. You're entirely dependent on memory.

During an OBE, you can't take notes, so you're forced to rely on your memory of the experience and the information you've obtained. For that reason, it's easier to identify simple, single targets than many targets or complex targets.

Problem 9. What constitutes proof?

Even if I could tell you things I "saw" at John's house, you could still write it off as "coincidence," "trickery," "cheating," and so on. Even if you could rule out these things, you couldn't rule out other psychic means of acquiring the information such as remote viewing, ESP, clairvoyance, telepathy, and so on.

Until science devises controlled laboratory experiments with short-distance targets, it will be very difficult to prove the objective reality of OBEs. The best proof is to try it yourself.

22

HOW OBE IS LIKE
TIGHTROPE WALKING

"What is love?" I asked my inner voice.
"Love is the carrier signal of the universe."
—Inner Voice

People are always asking me to explain how to leave the body. They want a simple, organized, fool-proof procedure for inducing out-of-body experiences. I remember a time when I wanted the same thing.

Reproducibility is the key to scientific proof, but most physicists know that reproducibility breaks down when you work at the quantum level, and perhaps it's even harder at the astral level. People think that it should be as easy as following a set of instructions or a recipe. Maybe it is easy for some people who have a natural talent for OBEs, but I don't have that natural talent, and neither do the people who ask me for help. I had to learn it all the hard way, through trial and error. OBEs are not predictable; there are many vari-ables that influence the experience.

Although it may or may not be related, there is a good analogy between OBEs and the firing of certain neurons in the brain. If I asked you to activate a particular cluster of neurons in the temporal lobe of your brain, you wouldn't know how, yet you've had years of experience doing it. The problem is that describing how to do it can be more difficult than doing it.

So how do you induce an OBE? An analogous question is: "How do you get to the other side of a tightrope?" I could describe the technique itself: place one foot directly in front of the other until you reach the other side, but there's more to it than that. I could describe the proper state of mind, the need to remain calm and collected, and not to panic. I could even try to describe the proper attire, what kind of shoes to wear, and so on. Even that's not enough information. I could describe how to balance, but that's more of a subjective thing, and not easily described. Even after you have all that information, you would still need to practice to develop the skill.

There is only one way to walk a tightrope, but there are many ways to achieve OBE. Hundreds of books have been written about OBEs, and many of them contain techniques for achieving it. It would be a major undertaking to present a comprehensive list of techniques. There are no guarantees of success, and one person's technique may not work for someone else. To complicate matters, there's more to it than the technique itself: it helps to have the proper environment, frame of mind, discipline.

Equipment and Setup

If you want to be successful at fishing, you need certain equipment: boat, motor, fishing rod, reel, fishing line, bait, and so forth. If you want to be successful at OBE, you need certain "equipment" too. The equipment for OBEs is less complex than that required for fishing. The important thing is to minimize all inputs from your physical senses.

To prevent touch distractions, make sure you have a comfortable place to practice (other than your bedroom, if possible[22]), comfortable clothes, a comfortable pillow. You should also make sure that you're not cutting off proper blood circulation.

To prevent visual distractions, you can do any or all of the following: close your eyes, pull the shades or drapes to keep excess sunlight out, wear an eye mask that blocks out light. Some experiments in parapsychology used ping-pong balls cut in half as makeshift eyewear to create a uniform visual field.

To prevent noise distractions, unplug the telephone, close the windows, wear earplugs, or listen to taped white noise to block out other sounds.

Most people aren't distracted by smells or tastes during OBE practice, but occasionally, you may be distracted by smells with strong associations, such as the smell of cookies baking, bacon frying, etc. If this is a concern, mask the smell with incense.

Sometimes it's impossible to cut off all input from your physical senses. For example, if you've been injured or sick, you may have pain that's impossible to eliminate. If you live in the middle of a large city, you

---

[22] We are all subconsciously programmed out of habit to fall asleep when we reach a certain location (your bed) and lie down at a certain time (at night). You will be more successful when you practice OBE techniques from a location other than your bedroom, and at a time other than the evening.

may not be able to eliminate traffic noise. If you have to live with distractions, learn how to ignore them. For example, one method I used to practice blocking out distractions was to deliberately fall asleep with heavy-metal music playing through headphones.

Location

If you're fishing in the wrong location, you can spend all day long without catching a single walleye. Similarly, choosing the right location to practice your OBEs will increase your chances of success. Your practice location should be quiet, dark, and comfortable, with as few distractions as possible. You can use a comfortable chair, couch, or bed, but ideally it should not be the one in your bedroom, for reasons already noted.

Technique

Leaving your body involves a certain type of meditation. There are many meditation techniques, but very few of these will lead to an OBE. Most techniques involve relaxing your body, focusing your mind inward, turning your attention away from the external senses, and focusing on internal events. Chapter 26 contains a simple procedure for inducing an OBE.

Mind-Set

It's important to have the right mind-set going into any situation. If you're nervous, you had better not try tightrope walking. If you're anxious, you probably shouldn't go fishing. Likewise, when you practice

OBEs, you should be calm, tranquil, and single-minded. You should eliminate all the noisy chatter inside your head: "I wonder what's going to happen. . . . I'm hungry. . . . What am I doing wrong?"

How to Be Successful

When you're trying to achieve an OBE, you have to hold your consciousness in a specific delicate state of balance for a period of time, much like walking a tightrope. If you can maintain the balance of your consciousness long enough, you can safely reach the other side. Once you've reached the other side, you can let go of that balance and explore the out-of-body state, just as if you've crossed the tightrope. But every time you lose that delicate balance before you reach your destination, like the performer falling off the tightrope, you have to start all over from the beginning.

You learn to induce OBEs in the same way a tightrope walker learns his or her skill. Your OBE success rate will in part depend on how often you practice. You practice it over and over, never giving up. You fall countless times into the safety net, and have to start all over again. Each time you make an attempt, you get an inch or two farther before you fall. Then one day you make it safely to the other side, and you congratulate yourself, but that doesn't make you an expert. You have to keep trying it, falling countless more times before you're successful again. After years of practice you can safely walk the thin line of consciousness (the tightrope) most of the time without falling. Then you can call yourself a successful astral traveler.

23

OBEs AND PSYCHIC PROTECTION

"What's today's lesson?" I asked my inner voice.
"Today, stop every once in a while and imagine
your vibrations are getting higher and higher, and
*   with it,*
feel an intense love build inside for All That Is."

There are many books about out-of-body experiences with many different approaches, from the scientific to the occult. Many of these books give the reader stern warnings against trying it for fear of death, disease, possession, insanity, heart attack, and even the fear of being mistaken for dead and buried alive. These notions of what can go wrong usually serve to instill the reader with fear, which in turn makes the problem worse. Since beliefs are more easily manifested in the astral world, your own negative beliefs can influence OBEs to be negative. Fear can attract malign entities. So it's important to know the facts and be able to protect yourself and not leave yourself open to attack.

Are OBEs Dangerous?

Many things in life are dangerous. Driving a car is dangerous. Crossing the street is dangerous. We do those things anyway. Sometimes walking into a danger-ous situation is our best course of action. In her book *Out-of-Body Experiences*, Janet Mitchell presents the fol-lowing analogy: "My parents did not keep me from walk-ing or tell me that I couldn't, even though they knew I might accidentally walk in front of a moving vehicle; they did teach me how to cross the street safely."

I'm not saying we should walk blindly into the street; I am saying that if we look both ways, we can safely nav-igate the out-of-body experience and add a new dimen-sion to our lives. In other words, "No guts, no glory."

What Are People Afraid Of?

Trying to induce an OBE can be very frightening, especially when you start getting results. You are faced with two of mankind's greatest fears:

Fear 1: Fear of the unknown.
Fear 2: Fear of death.

Both of these fears are driven by our instincts. Because humans are mammals, we have a natural instinct to survive and that instinct makes us respond with fear to situations where we are in unfamiliar ter-ritory (OBEs qualify). Once you realize that millions of people have had OBEs without any problems, it's eas-ier to accept OBEs as relatively safe, or at least not life-threatening.

Once those fears are conquered, there are "pokes and prods" that may startle you during practice. I wrote about them in my first book, but I left the issue unre-solved. I discovered that the pokes and prods were either fears of mine being manifested or astral entities trying to help me out of my body (or possibly trying to discourage me from leaving it). In either case, I worked through the fear, and since I did that, I no longer get poked during practice. Well, maybe just on rare occasions.

Fear 3: Not being able to get back in.

Some people are afraid that they might not be able to get back inside their body once they've left it. Obviously, there's no way to prove this can't happen, because if it has happened to anyone, they've not lived to tell us about it. I can, however, speak from experience: I've never had a problem getting back into my body. Usually I get sucked back in automatically when my body wants attention. The problem is not getting back in, but how to stay out longer, how to prolong the experience.

On a related topic, many people have frequent episodes of an experience known as "false awakening" that makes it *seem* as though they can't get back inside their body (see chapter 19). False awakening experi-ences may be terrifying until you understand what's happening. Your mind wakes up while your physical body is still disabled by sleep paralysis, a natural mech-anism that keeps you from thrashing in your sleep. Sometimes it can take several minutes before your physical body catches up with the mind.

Fear 4: Death due to severing the silver cord.

Throughout history, people from all cultures have reported seeing a silver cord connecting the astral body to the physical body. The most notable quotation is from the Bible: "Before the silver cord is snapped" (Ecclesiastes 12:6). Some authors warn against tampering with your silver cord during an OBE. They state that tampering with the cord can result in disease, injury, or even death. It's understandable that people should be concerned about keeping the silver cord safe from harm, but only if the silver cord is a "real" (objective) thing.

Some habitual astral travelers have never seen their own silver cord, even when they look for it. This fact leads some researchers to conclude the cord is not an objective phenomenon but rather a psychological one. Other researchers insist the silver cord is "real" and point out that a silver cord has been reported not only by out-of-body experiencers, but also by people witnessing seances and deaths:

> These "silver cords" were not imagined: in the first place, some (namely, those of certain materializations) have been photographed; in the second place, some were seen collectively; in the third place, dozens of people in different circumstances do not imagine the same things—or their occurrence in the same series of events. These "cords" were objective phenomena, extensions between the vacated physical body and the released, objective "double" (Crookall 1970, p. 167).

I've experienced the silver cord phenomenon firsthand. In my first book, I described some humorous OBEs where I played tug-of-war with my seemingly real silver cord, and lost. Despite this, I tend to side with the first camp in thinking that the silver cord is merely a creation of my own mind. In my experiences, I never came to any harm, no matter how roughly I handled the cord.

Even if the cord is "real," I don't believe it can be harmed during an OBE because it seems to be made of purely astral matter. People have flown through high-voltage power lines, which should have affected the silver cord as they passed through, if it were made of physical or even semiphysical material.

The silver cord doesn't seem to have a distance limitation, either. Sylvan Muldoon tried to test the limits of the silver cord and concluded that its "elasticity is far beyond the imagination, and is not comparable to any material object in its stretching qualities" (Muldoon and Carrington 1970, p. 77). Other OBEers have "flown" thousands of miles across oceans and even into outer space, leading some to conclude that the silver cord has no limits to its elasticity.

My experience has led me to believe that OBEs are not harmful to the physical body or mind in any way, but there are no guarantees of safety. Obviously, if anyone has died during an OBE, they haven't been able to come back and warn us about the danger.

Fear 5: Getting lost or losing your body.

When you're out of your body, you can fly anywhere, even into outer space. You can cross into different levels of astral reality, where "dead" people live. Naturally some people worry it's possible to get lost and not be able to find your body again. It is possible to be "lost" during an OBE, but it's not a problem because you can always get back to your body. I've had many OBEs where I found myself in some strange house and had no idea where I was. I don't think it's possible to lose your body. I've been doing this for twenty years now, and I've never had a problem getting back to my body, no matter how "lost" I was. I've had the telephone ring while I was having an OBE, and it brought me back to my body with a violent and unpleasant "slam."

Some people think that the silver cord is used to pull you back inside your body in case of an emergency. Some people believe that the silver cord is merely a creation of the mind, citing the fact that very few people actually report any cord (Blackmore 1992, p. 22). Regardless of whether the silver cord is involved, there *is* a built-in mechanism that will always pull you back to your body if the need arises. My theory is that some portion of your soul—maybe your oversoul or higher self—monitors what's happening to your body while you're away, and forces your return when it needs to. I don't know how this is accomplished, but in my experience, you are always returned to your body.

Fear 6: Spirits harming your body or soul.

To address the concern over spirits harming you, you must first examine the issue of "spirits" in general and whether they can be trusted. As I said in chapter 5, dying doesn't necessarily make a person better than they were when they were alive.

Some spirits don't realize they've died, and some of them may desperately try to contact you. They may try harder and harder to get your attention because ordinary in-the-body people don't see them and they don't like being ignored. These people usually hold onto their dense vibrations so tightly that they can't even see the spirit helpers and guides who surround them, waiting to take them to the light, but they can usually see another person who has density, someone who still has a connection to the Earth and whose vibrations aren't quite so high—like someone having an OBE. Therefore, many OBE adepts are employed as astral rescue workers to convince Earth-bound souls to get the help they need to get on with their nonphysical life. Sometimes it's enough to simply tell them they've passed on and they should look for a spirit to help them find their way.

Once spirits realize they're dead, they won't bother you because they are either (a) wrapped up in non-physical worlds and therefore not interested in you or (b) guardian angels who accepted the job of watching over the living. The trick is not to attract their attention. Some religious fanatics believe so strongly in their "Satan" and "evil" that they attract negative entities. They believe in the power of evil, so they *empower* evil to work. Also, their fear of these evil powers causes them to have negative experiences. If they truly believed that they were protected by God, and higher forces (which they are), such things would not happen to them. Some of these fanatics successfully drive away negative entities by invoking the name of Jesus Christ, even in cases where the spirit does not share their Christian beliefs. Their power is in their faith. Jesus knew that faith was the key. A Buddhist, Taoist, or other religious devotee with as much faith could do the same. If you believe that an entity can hurt you, then you empower it; however, if you believe that you are protected, then you will be. If you have conflicting beliefs, then usually good will win.

In general, spirit entities can't really harm you physically. They can mess with your mind, but only by using deception and illusions. They can control you only through fear, so fearlessness is the best protection in the world. "The only thing you have to fear is fear itself." Most people don't realize how much power they have; therefore, they let themselves be controlled by fear, but if you realize your power, you can wield it.

I receive e-mail from around the world, and I'm often asked about psychic protection. One person wrote, "Forget about the dead people; that's only part of the problem. There are demons, fallen angels, aliens, snakes, spiders, and other astral beings who attach themselves to humans unbeknownst to them. The number of negative entities in the astral world is commensurate with the number of potentially pathogenic organisms in the world. It is a zoo, and the best time for them to attack is when the body is left unattended."

It is true that there are malign entities in the astral world, just as there are poisonous plants and deadly animals in this world. Belief creates reality in the astral world, so if you believe in multitudes of negative entities, you will create them and/or invite them into your life. If you believe it is a "zoo" then it will be. That's why it is important to conquer your fears and critically examine your belief system before attempting OBEs. I personally don't believe in demons or fallen angels. Other nonhuman astral entities (including aliens and other creatures) have a path of spiritual evolution, just as we do. They may have different motivations from humans, but they are a part of nature, and as such, they are not "evil."

Some people believe that we enter the astral world with no protection at all. They might insist that malign entities can harm us because they are not afraid of racking up more "bad karma" (The Hindu and

Buddhist belief that our actions, both good and bad, affect what happens to us in the future. In Christian terms, "As you sow, so shall you reap."), whereas angels can't help us because it would be "violating our free will." I believe we are all creatures of God playing by the same rules. If the laws of free will prevent angels from helping us, they also prevent malign entities from harming us. If, however, these creatures can violate free will to harm us, then so can angels to help us to the same degree. If you believe that angels will not violate free will to help you in times of need, use your free will to invoke their help: pray or call out to them for help.

I'm not saying that bad things can't happen during an OBE. To facilitate a life-lesson, some people may have pre-existing subconscious agreements with negative entities which may be harmful, but we also have pre-existing agreements with angels which can be equally helpful. Your higher self will ensure that nothing will happen that is not part of your life-lessons.

If the unfamiliar territory of OBEs makes you uncomfortable, play it safe. In this world, most people don't normally confront dangerous animals because they try to stay out of harm's way. Likewise, if you stick to safer areas during OBEs, you shouldn't have a problem. If you find yourself in a dark, dreary place during an OBE, or if you find yourself surrounded by hostile entities, you should abort the experience and try again later. The best way to do that is to think about your physical body, and you will be automatically pulled back inside it.

I believe that every one of us is comprised of God's being, and therefore, we have unlimited power. Once you realize your power and learn to wield it through practice, you can conquer any astral foe. The key is to believe in yourself. Therefore, I'd rather instill you with a sense of power and fearlessness, because, in my experience, that is what creates your protection.

When I have an OBE, I am fearless. I dare any astral entity to mess with me. I'll kick its ass, and it knows it. Call me naive, but I think that ordinary in-the-body people should have that fearless attitude toward attackers and rapists, too. Most rapists use fear to control their victims and if the victim reacts by fighting and screaming, resisting and refusing to give up that control, the attacker will usually flee.

Some people believe that there are guardian angels that will watch over your body while you're away. You probably won't even notice them because their higher vibrations may render them invisible, just as most people don't see ultraviolet light.

I also believe that some portion of our higher self watches over our body during an OBE and keeps it from harm. Your higher self, which is more powerful than you can imagine, has invested several years of your life creating your body for a collection of life experiences and unless your life is through, it's not about to give up your physical body.

Fear 7: Demonic possession.

Demonic possession has been reported throughout written history. It's not surprising that some people are concerned about it. There are several reasons why you shouldn't be worried about possession. I don't know if there are any studies showing possession statistics, but I believe the majority of "possessions" reported in the last two thousand years were not demonic possession, but rather, either a physiological problem such as

Tourette's syndrome,[23] rabies, or else a psychological problem such as dissociative disorder (also known as multiple personality disorder,[24] or MPD) or schizophrenia. Until the twentieth century, people with Tourette's and MPD were usually thought of as demonically possessed. Today, psychologists and doctors understand mental illnesses and brain diseases a lot better, eliminating most of the superstition.

In my first book, I mentioned that I don't believe in "evil"; therefore, I don't believe that "demons" are a force of organized evil, as most Christians believe.

I mentioned that I believe there are two kinds of demons. The first kind of "demon" is the kind we create in our own minds. They are usually a manifestation of a deeply rooted belief that OBE is somehow wrong. These "demons" may be created subconsciously to deter you from inducing the OBEs if you believe deep down that it is wrong. A common variation of this experience is when people hear voices ordering them to "stop" or "go back." Others hear their wife, mother, or an authority figure calling them to "wake up" during

---

[23] Named after French doctor Georges Gilles de la Tourette, Tourette's syndrome is a chronic, physical disorder of the brain that causes both motor tics and vocal tics (often with foul language), and typically begins before the age of eighteen.

[24] Sensationalized by movies like *The Three Faces of Eve* and books like *Sybil*, this psychiatric condition is a dissociative disorder where one person has two or more distinct personalities, each personality having a distinct and consistent pattern of relating to self and the environment. At least two of these personalities recurrently take full control of the person's behavior. MPD may occur in 1 percent of the population (Sidran Foundation 1994).

OBE attempts, but when they snap out of it, there is no one there. The person who was calling was a creation of their own subconscious mind.

The second kind of demon is a spirit that is playing the role of a demon. This kind of "demon" is really just an astral entity who is no different from you or me, but they're impersonating a demon. Maybe they're trying to intimidate or frighten you, but they are impostors nonetheless. Like any stranger you meet on the street, the entity might be benign or malign. They may have good or bad intentions, but they can only possess your physical body while you're away if you give them permission to, or if you're frightened enough to give up control of your body.

As long as you remain fearless, they cannot harm your body and they can't steal your body. Even if they could control your body, they couldn't hold onto it for long. Once again, your body's automatic "pull-back" mechanism comes into play. If some entity disturbs your physical body while you are away, you will automatically be pulled back inside before it can do any harm.

What Are the Real Dangers?

What can a malicious entity do to you? Hurt you physically? Not good enough: If I were afraid of physical pain, I wouldn't drive my car every day. (And most women wouldn't have babies.) Can they invade your body? Not unless it's part of your life-lesson. Can they take away or imprison your soul? No way.

Most of the danger is from within. People who are unstable may just come unglued because of OBEs. People who are unwary or gullible may let some spirit with ill-intent talk them or trick them into giving up control, inviting possession, and so forth. If you are strong, spiritual, and connected to God, then you have nothing to worry about. People who don't understand the rules of astral travel and can't control their fears may create their own "demons" to torment them. It's not for timid or foolish people.

Fears Are Detrimental—Discard Them

Anytime we face the unknown, it can be frightening. But approaching anything with fear is harmful. Early European sailors believed the Earth was flat and they could sail off the edge. Because of their fear of the unknown, they concluded it was dangerous to sail too far West. When they conquered their fear and went bravely ahead, not only did they discover a new world, they also made the transition from two-dimensional thinking to three-dimensional thinking about their reality. Likewise, if we can conquer our fears, we will also discover a whole new world, and we will make the transition from three-dimensional thinking to four-or-more-dimensional thinking about our reality.

All the great pioneers have set aside their fears, at least temporarily, and gone ahead despite the dangers. Courage is not the ability to walk into danger without fear. Courage is the ability to walk into a dangerous or frightening situation and think to yourself, "Yes, I'm scared—I'm scared to death—but that's not going to stop me."

How to Handle Malign Entities

If you encounter negative entities during an OBE, there are several strategies you can use to safely handle the situation.

Strategy 1: Return to your body.

The first strategy is also the simplest if you meet up with negative entities during an OBE: Simply drop back into your body. This is the safest and simplest way to escape bad OBE situations, but you also forfeit your chance to explore.

Strategy 2: Surround yourself with a protective light.

One good strategy for dealing with danger is to imagine an opaque barrier or wall of protective white light surrounding you. This works to keep all entities from coming near you because powerful thoughts often become reality in the astral world. Also, imagine a "Do Not Disturb" message that will be encountered by all who try to reach you. Although protecting yourself with the light seems like a short-term temporary solution, it need not be. If you wield your power of protection well enough, and with enough consistency, you will eventually convince negative entities that they can no longer get to you. You can even inform the entity that it's no use trying to attack you, because you will *always* have a defense; therefore, it's wasting its time. Incidentally, this method of protection works to keep entities from bothering you while you're inside your body too.

Strategy 3: Turn your power against the attacker.

Since entities typically use fear as their weapon, one strategy is to turn the tables on your attacker. The best defense is a strong offense. You can get angry and scream at the entity to leave you alone, or else you will kick its butt. Threaten to cause it more pain than it ever thought possible. Most entities are frightened by the power we possess as incarnates.

Strategy 4: Respond with love.

Try feeling as much love as you can for these misguided souls. The feelings of love will have multiple benefits. The love will drive away all fear, robbing the entity of its power over you. It will also raise your vibrations to a level where the entity can't reach you and create a protective energy all around you.

When we travel out-of-body, we are exploring uncharted territory. Obviously, no one can guarantee your safety during an OBE, so please use caution and common sense when exploring.

24

ARE ALIEN ABDUCTIONS OBEs?

*"When you focus on the hole, you see the hole.
When you focus on the whole, you see the
whole."*

—Inner Voice

Suppose that your best friend tells you of a strange experience that happened last night. Shortly after she went to bed, she noticed a strange, bright white light fill her bedroom. She felt a bit odd. Then she noticed a strange hissing sound, and her body began to vibrate, almost as if she were being electrocuted. She felt paralyzed, unable to move, terrified. Next, some kind of strange being who had a luminescent glow seemed to just walk through the bedroom wall. Then she started floating up in the air, seeming to defy gravity itself. She floated toward a wall, but instead of hitting the wall, she seemed to go through it. The next thing she knew, she was in a strange room she didn't recognize. That being of light talked to her, and told her that humanity is destroying the environment, and that she has a special purpose to fulfill. The next thing she knew, she was waking up in bed again. Was this an alien abduction or an out-of-body experience? Actually, it could be either.

In this chapter, I will compare the features of out-of-body experiences with features of alien abduction experiences. There are hundreds of books on OBEs, but for this chapter, most of the information on OBEs is taken from Gabbard and Twemlow's book, *With the Eyes of the Mind: An Empirical Analysis of Out-of-Body States*.

I don't pretend to be a scholar in the field of UFOs. I first became interested in the similarities between OBEs and alien abductions because of several conversations I had with my sister-in-law, who is a member of the Mutual UFO Network (MUFON), a citizen-based group that studies UFO-related topics. When she described the common features of alien abductions, I was intrigued by how similar they were to the features of out-of-body experiences. My initial thought was "I wonder how many people think they're having alien abductions, but they're just having OBEs?" I don't know if other comparisons have been done between the two phenomena, but I thought it was worth studying. Given the ability to distinguish between the two, some people might find it comforting to know that their disturbing experiences are related to OBEs instead of aliens.

The information I am using on alien abductions comes mainly from *Abduction* by John Mack, M.D., with the page numbers cited coming from the 1995 paperback edition. I hold the greatest admiration for John Mack and the work he has done, and in no way do I mean to imply anything negative about him or his research. I'm using his book as a point of reference in this chapter because it was convenient. I had the privilege of hearing Mack speak at a MUFON symposium in July 1996 in Greensboro, North Carolina. What impressed me most was his approach to the alien abduction phenomenon, particularly his genuine concern for the people affected. UFO research is a field of study that normally puts more emphasis on facts, figures, and empirical evidence, yet Mack talked about a spiritual approach to the phenomenon that puts humanity before facts and figures. He seemed not as concerned with proving the reality of the abduction phenomenon as he was about how the experience affected people.

I have two reasons for writing this chapter: First, I want to encourage future research concerning the similarities between the two phenomena by experts from both fields. Second, I want to help clinicians and patients more accurately distinguish between the two. It's not my intention to insist that OBEs and alien abductions are the same thing. Although there are startling similarities, there are also significant differences. I will discuss the differences as well as the similarities.

Features Common to OBEs

First, let's look at the features of a typical out-of-body experience. The table below is a brief summary of features common to OBEs, as reported by Gabbard and Twemlow (p. 19). Next to each feature is a percentage that represents how frequently the OBE feature is reported in some surveys.

No.	Common Features of OBEs	%
1.	Experience was more real than a dream	94
2.	OBE body similar to physical body	76
3.	Same environment as physical body	62
4.	Felt a sense of energy	55
5.	Wanted to return to body	54
6.	Felt able to pass through objects	50

7.	Felt vibrations in body	38
8.	Part of awareness was still in body	37
9.	Was aware of presence of beings	37
10.	Heard noises in early stages	37
11.	Experienced a change in time sense	33
12.	Saw a brilliant white light	30
13.	Felt the presence of guides or helpers	26
14.	Dark tunnel with white light at end	26
15.	Felt attached to physical body	21
16.	Felt able to touch objects	18
17.	Felt that others were aware of them	14
18.	Felt a sense of border or limit	14
19.	Experienced panoramic vision	14

Now let's look closer at Gabbard and Twemlow's list of features common to OBEs, and compare them to features of alien abductions. All page numbers in the examples refer to Mack's *Abduction*.

Experience was more real than a dream

A large number of people who have out-of-body experiences (94%) say that the experience was more real than a dream. A lot of attention has been given to this fact in the OBE literature. Examples of this may be found in the OBE case histories documented by Robert Crookall and others, in which subjects don't realize they are having an OBE until they happen to see their own physical body lying inanimate on the bed. In fact, I think it's safe to assume that many of these OBE subjects would not have realized their OBE state had it not been for seeing their own body, or otherwise having experienced something that is not common to physical life, such as floating or passing through physical objects.

Alien abductions are also viewed as more real than a dream; in fact, abductions are commonly viewed as having occurred physically (as opposed to nonphysically, "astrally," or whatever). Occasionally, abductions are described as having a dreamlike or hazy quality. Perhaps this is an indication that the subject was fully conscious (as can occur in OBEs, lucid dreams, and other altered states of consciousness), but that the reality didn't seem up to the standards of everyday physical life.

Examples:

Subject Ed reported his experiences as having a "misty quality" (p. 42). Sheila described hers as "electrical dreams" and "spiritual dreams" (p. 55). Catherine said, "It seems more real than a dream, but not as real as me talking to you" (p. 142).

OBE body similar to physical body

Gabbard and Twemlow found that 76% of OBE subjects report that their body image during an OBE was very similar or identical to their physical body. Many OBE subjects report that the astral body can defy gravity and seems ghostlike. Later, I will discuss the occasional cases where the subject's astral body takes a form different from their physical body. During alien abductions, subjects believe their experiences to be physical. Subjects report physical examinations, experiments, and even surgeries performed on their bodies. Obviously they experience their bodies as similar to their normal physical bodies. In some cases, abductees also report their bodies as ghostlike.

Example:

Subject Carlos: "The body just dissolves and goes up. Then I am transparent. I have a sense of the interior transparent shell of the body which is not part of its physicality but yet it is connected. It is the shape of the physicality . . . The molecular structure, cellular structure of the body, just goes out into the light . . . It is the transformation from one state of being into another state of being, but you carry the core of a residual shape . . . it is like a ghost image. The image is the memory of the body, and it is clear and it is there and it has form" (p. 349).

Same environment as physical body

Most OBEs seem to take place in an environment almost identical or at least very similar to the physical one. Most OBEs occur in subjects' bedrooms, at least at the onset of the experience. During the OBE, subjects see all the normal physical surroundings they expect to see where their physical bodies were last located. If they were in their bedroom, they often see their bed, dressers, closets, and so forth during the OBE. Later, the environment may change to other more exotic environments such as grandiose meeting halls or heavenly surroundings.

Most abductions seem to take place in the same physical environment as well. Abductions often take place in subjects' bedrooms, and subjects also see their normal physical environment at the onslaught of the experience. Later, subjects are somehow transported to another, more exotic environment, that of an alien ship.

Felt a sense of energy

In more than half the OBEs studied by Gabbard and Twemlow (55%), subjects reported having a sense of energy. Alien abductees also describe a feeling of energy. *Example:*

Subject Sheila described her experiences as "full of electricity" (p. 56).

Wanted to return to body (end the experience)

Fifty-four percent of OBE subjects wanted to return to their bodies, or otherwise bring the experience to an end. Alien abductees also report wanting to end the experience.

Example:

Subject Peter yelled, "I want this to stop" (p. 304).

Felt able to pass through objects

During OBEs, it's very common for the subject to seemingly pass through physical matter. There are hundreds of cases where the subject has reached for a doorknob, and their hand goes right through it. To get to the next room, they typically discover they can walk through the door, or even a wall. Floating through the ceiling, or through the floor, is also common during OBEs.

In alien abduction experiences, it's very common for subjects to describe being lifted up into the air, and passing through walls, windows, and even windows with bars on them. Aliens are also described as having walked through walls or locked doors, as if transcending the solidness of matter.

Examples:

Subject Catherine floated "literally through" the front door (p. 135). Subject Paul felt "himself pass literally through the door of the ship" (p. 225). Subject Peter said: "It's not the same as like physically walking through a wall. It's like stepping into an energy field. . . . They didn't carry me through that wall this time. I walked through it" (p. 312).

Felt vibrations in body

Many OBEers have described feeling a strong, electrical type of vibration or "buzzing" that courses through their body during the process of separating from it. This has been described by such famous authors as Robert Monroe. According to Monroe and others, the vibrations can range from coarse and rough to smooth to almost unnoticeable. Some authors have theorized that separation from the body occurs when the vibrations of the spiritual body are increased to a point where the physical body gets out of synchronization or can no longer hold on to the astral body. Alien abduction subjects may also experience a type of electrical vibration at the beginning of the experience.

Examples:

Subject Ed reported a "tingling sensation" at the base of his skull (p. 43). Scott reported "buzzing" in his right ear that changed to a ringing sound, and said, "I lost control of my body" (p. 86). Jerry heard "buzzing and ringing and whirring" noises in her head (p. 106). Sara had "electrical sensations in her body" on one occasion (p. 194). Dave reported "a vibration of some kind, a tingling" (p. 261). Peter said, "I remember my whole body vibrated and shook maybe for a second, two seconds, three seconds" (p. 289).

Part of awareness was still in body

Some OBE subjects (37%) experienced some kind of dual consciousness, where they seemed to retain some sort of awareness of their physical body as well as the nonphysical body. During alien abductions, subjects can also experience a sense of dual consciousness. I will discuss this in the section labeled "Sense of separation from physical body."

Was aware of presence of beings

The same number of OBE subjects (37%) said they were aware of the presence of other beings, often reported as "non-physical" beings. During an alien abduction experience, the subject typically sees and interacts with "alien beings." It is interesting to note that the books written about OBEs contain almost no mention of aliens, extraterrestrials, or UFOs. I can only assume that they've never seen alien creatures during their OBEs or else they're afraid of losing credibility if they write about them. I haven't seen aliens in my OBEs.

Heard noises in early stages

Another 37% of OBE experiencers heard strange accompanying noises at the early stages of the OBE. This often seems to be related to the vibrations that are described as running through their body. Usually these noises are described as loud, rattling, roaring, or deafening. Once the separation from the body is complete, the noises usually go away and are not noticed any more. Just as the vibrations can be soft, hard, or unnoticeable, so too the noises that accompany them can be soft, loud, or unnoticeable. Alien abductees often describe hearing noises as well, usually during the early stages of the experience.

Examples:

Subject Sheila reported "hearing a very loud, high-pitched noise" (p. 66). Peter said, "I can hear the vibration" (p. 296).

Experienced a change in time sense

OBE subjects often say that their sense of time becomes distorted during their experiences. Some people describe it as if time had stopped for them. During alien abduction experiences, subjects may also feel a distorted sense of time; hence the term, "missing time" in UFO literature.

Example:

Subject Peter "experienced the collapse of past, present, and future" (p. 327).

Saw a brilliant light

Thirty percent of the OBE subjects reported seeing a brilliant light during the experience. Although I don't have the exact figures, this percentage is higher among people who have experienced OBEs as part of a near-death experience (NDE). This has even been made famous by books such as *Embraced by the Light* by Betty Eadie. Alien abductions often include bright lights as well.

Examples:

Subject Sheila described a "blinking red light 'coming in all the windows all over the place'" (p. 66). Scott was "awed by the intensity and brilliance of the light he had seen while on the table" (p. 87). Peter experienced a "loss of control as light filled the room and he felt a 'presence' around his bed" (p. 289). Arthur said, "It was the most incredible light. If there is such a thing as pure white. Totally pure, and it was everywhere" (p. 370).

Felt the presence of guides or helpers

During OBEs, 26% of the people felt the presence of guides or helpers. These are often thought of as spirit guides or friends. During alien abductions, the aliens are sometimes described as guides or helpers.

Examples:

Aliens showed Catherine scenes from a past life and taught her lessons about getting rid of fear (pp.

161–62). Mack wrote, "The alien beings . . . appear to have been with, or at least available to, [Joe] as protectors and guides of his spiritual evolution over time" (p. 190). Mack also wrote, "The alien beings function as spirit energies or guides, serving the evolution of consciousness and identity" (p. 255).

Dark tunnel with white light at end

Twenty-six percent of the OBE subjects described moving through a dark tunnel that had a white light at the end. Sometimes abductees also report this effect or similar effects.

Examples:

Subject Ed reported "going down this time tunnel" (p. 44). Carlos described a "laserlike tunnel of light" (p. 345).

Felt attached to physical body

In 21% of the OBE subjects, the subject reported having some kind of connection or attachment to the physical body. Sometimes this is described as the silver cord. In most abduction cases, since the subject doesn't believe they are out of their body, they don't feel any kind of connection to it. However, there are some exceptions.

Example:

Subject Paul was connected through his back by "cords" (p. 224).

Felt able to touch objects

Eighteen percent of OBE subjects felt that they were able to touch objects. In abduction cases, subjects are also able to touch objects. More often, they feel the touch of "medical" devices during invasive procedures.

Felt that others were aware of them

Fourteen percent of OBE subjects felt that people not out-of-body were aware of their presence. In abduction cases, subjects usually feel the aliens are aware of their presence.

Felt a sense of border or limit

Fourteen percent of OBE subjects felt a sense of border or limit. In abduction cases, subjects also feel a sense of border or limit. They see walls of the space-craft they are in, for example.

Experienced panoramic vision

Fourteen percent of OBE subjects experienced panoramic vision. I haven't come across alien abductions that describe true panoramic vision, but something similar to it, instead.

Example:

Subject Carlos described "looking out the window as I walked around the circular space, and I was seeing this beautiful paradise, Earth, in every direction" (p. 363).

Other Symptoms Common to Both Alien Abductions and OBEs

There are other striking similarities between OBEs and alien abductions. Although the following symptoms are not categorized in Gabbard and Twemlow's book, these symptoms are common to most OBEs, and are documented in other books, such as those by Robert Crookall.

Sense of separation from physical body

Most people presume that OBEs and alien abductions are unrelated, yet I was surprised to find several references to OBEs in *Abduction*. It would seem that alien abductees are particularly prone to having OBEs. Other cases have a distinct sense of separation of consciousness, but are not spoken of as an OBE.

Examples:

Mack wrote: "At some point Scott had a kind of out-of-body experience from fear, as he looked down on himself and saw his head on a blocklike pillow" (p. 86). Jerry "told several churchmen about an out-of-body experience she had had" (p. 109). Joe said he "would just go out of" himself and go "anywhere" to "world, space, planets, distance." When Mack asked him, "Your body or your consciousness or both?" Joe replied, "Without my body, sometimes in my body. I become wind. I become space. I become matter. I spin, swirl, slow, fall" (p. 173). Sara said, "I felt like I got out of my body and I couldn't get back in, and I was gone for about two days" (p. 194). Eva saw herself floating from the ceiling. She said, "My consciousness was up there. My physical body was down there" (p. 237). Peter experienced "consciousness being separate from my physical body, like up here, looking down at myself sitting at this table" (p. 314). Carlos "described what might have been an out-of-body experience during this illness in which he was visited once again by three or four little creatures with large eyes"(p. 339). Arthur's "consciousness seemed to split away somewhat" (p. 371).

Paralysis

At the onset of an out-of-body experience, the subject often feels paralyzed. Some researchers have explained this as being caused by sleep paralysis in the subject's body during the experience. During many alien abductions, subjects claim to have been somehow immobilized by the aliens, and unable to move, or even scream.

Examples:

"Jerry had a number of 'nightmares' in which she would awake paralyzed" (p. 106). Catherine "couldn't move at all" (p. 137). Paul "wanted to open his eyes but simply could not do it. He 'dozed off again' (a common paradox in abduction-related terror) and then upon awakening was able to 'break out of it' and look, but there was 'nothin' there.' Although fully conscious now, Paul found he was 'gagging on my breath because I couldn't speak' and was still unable to move for a few more minutes" (p. 213). Dave "was paralyzed now, able to move only his eyes" (p. 269). Peter said, "I'm paralyzed. I want to kill it, and I can't do anything" (p. 290).

Floating sensations, defying gravity

Subjects having an OBE typically are able to float and defy the laws of gravity. Often, subjects describe flying or gliding as well. Alien abductees claim a similar thing. Abductees commonly float up out of bed and are drawn up into an alien craft.

Examples:

Subject Ed talked about a "sensation of floating, and my whole body is starting to float" (p. 43). Peter floated "right through the window." Later, he "floated through the dining and kitchen area and out the door" (pp. 288, 291).

Sudden inexplicable changes in location or position

During an out-of-body experience, the subject is prone to sudden shifts in location. One minute it may seem as if the subject is lying in bed and the next minute, standing in a strange room. During an alien abduction, sudden and/or unexpected changes in location or position also occur.

Examples:

Subject Sheila "believes that she went to sleep lying on her left side, but the next thing she actually recalls was being awake on her back" (p. 66). She also describes lying in bed, and after describing. a white light, she says, "It doesn't look like my bedroom" (p. 67). Catherine said, "The room seemed to transform from a typically spare space-ship room with tables, curved walls, and perhaps a viewing screen into an ornate executive conference room complete with shag carpeting, mahogany paneling, and a large viewing screen" (p. 160). Mack wrote: "The positions of her [Eva's] body she found confusing. 'When I was aware of what was happening it was like I was on my side, but when it was happening, I was on my back'" (p. 242).

Thoughts instantly manifest reality/travel via thought power

Most OBE writers have talked about how thoughts can instantly manifest or bring about changes in reality. If the OBE subject thinks about their body, they are instantly zapped back into the body. If they think about floating, they start floating. Reality seems to bend itself around our thoughts but also seems limited to what we expect. It is also interesting to note that OBE subjects often speak of traveling via thought power: think of a place, and you will be transported there. These ideas also appear in some alien abductions.

Examples:

Mack wrote: "As Catherine recalled when she reviewed the tape of this session, she had had the impression that 'the more I thought of a corporate executive conference room, the more it appeared,' but when she realized that this was a kind of staging, the conference room 'images just melted away to reveal the previous images, and finally the actual room'" (p. 160). Mack also said, "Travel occurs when 'you just think yourself there'" (p. 175).

Telepathic communications

During OBEs, the subjects communicate telepathically with one another. During alien abductions, the subjects almost always communicate with their captors telepathically.

Examples:

Subject Catherine said, "He knows exactly what I'm thinking. He's answering the questions before I even think of them" (p. 151). Eva said she was "able to communicate telepathically with the entities" (p. 249). Mack also wrote, "Dave said he had talk [sic] with Master Joe about the possibility that the alien beings have mastered the capacity to communicate telepathically" (p. 273).

Increased wisdom, spirituality, and spiritual transformation

OBEs often lead to a kind of spiritual transformation. They often catalyze the individual into becoming more involved in religious pursuits, meditation, and other spiritual paths. OBEs that occur within a near-death experience seem to have an even greater impact. Alien abductions also lead to a similar kind of spiritual transformation. Many times, abductees are inspired to study spiritual paths.

Examples:

Subject Ed was noted to have practiced meditation and studied Eastern philosophy (p. 42). Jerry described a "profound transformational process" (p. 99). Catherine talked about "spiritual growth, this psychic growth" (p. 157).

Able to see their own body

It's common for the OBE subject to see their own physical body as another object in the room. There are cases of this in alien abduction literature, too.

Examples:

Joe said, "I feel like I just integrated all parts of me towards oneness." He also described "a powerful image of looking down and seeing his own body as if in 'a hall of mirrors' and saw himself 'on many different levels'" (p. 180). Peter said it was "as if his 'spirit' were up in the corner of the room, he could look down on his body on the bed" (pp. 311–12).

Increased psychic abilities

Some authors have documented a connection between out-of-body experiences and increased psychic abilities. Alien abductees have also reported increased psychic abilities.

Examples:

"Scott feels that his psychic powers have increased as a result of his experiences" (p. 96). Because of her experiences, Catherine can "feel people's auras" (p. 157). Sara "exhibited certain paranormal powers, such as the ability at least to create the impression of levitating another child" (p. 206). Mack also wrote, "Paul (like many abductees) has been psychically skilled all his life and seems to grow more so as he recovers memories of his alien encounters" (pp. 226–27).

Life flashes before eyes

One of the most common features of a near-death experience is subjects seeing their lives flash before their eyes. Surprisingly, this is sometimes reported in alien abductions.

Examples:

"Memories of his [Scott's] life flashed before him, as he felt had happened 'so many times' during abductions" (p. 86). Carlos sees "televised/projected imagery of a miniature holographic nature, in which particular and multiple personal life scenes are played out while he watches" (p. 349).

Lose consciousness and "wake up" at the end of the experience

A typical OBE ends when the subject loses consciousness, and "wakes up" in bed. A typical alien abduction ends when the subject loses consciousness and wakes up in bed.

Example:

Peter "awoke" at 11:05 at the end of an experience (p. 295).

Transcending space and time

During an OBE, the subjects often describe being able to transcend space and time. Some people have had experiences of traveling through time during OBEs, while others describe spanning vast distances of space in the blink of an eye. Some alien abductions also have these characteristics.

Examples:

Mack wrote, "As we reviewed the session, Catherine, like other abductees, suggested the things she had experienced 'are like not from our space/time'" (p. 163). Later he wrote, "Other projects are not Earth-related. and involve 'other dimensions, other galaxies,' but 'time and space is not an issue'" (p. 175).

Double life, other reality, other dimension, or other plane

Many people who have OBEs feel as if they are leading a double life, or a life that contains extracurricular activities beyond their daily waking lives. Most subjects feel their experiences are taking them to another reality, or a different dimension. In occult literature, this is also described as being on a different plane of existence, such as the astral plane, thus the term "astral travel." Alien abductees also talk about leading a double life. Abductees sometimes even describe their experiences in terms of a different reality.

Examples:

Subject Ed said he had "access into their dimension" (p. 51). Jerry said, "I then said, 'Well, if this is real then I am somehow living a double life.' . . . I had a feeling there was a definite reason that I and others like me were not aware of this other reality, at least not as aware as we are about this reality we have here and now" (p. 108). Concerning subject Sara, Mack wrote, "Despite the joy she feels when she enters the other dimension, Sara feels it would not have been 'ethically correct' for her to 'jump' the chasm between the two planes totally or too readily" (p. 205). Eva was "living two dimensions simultaneously . . . I have the gut feeling I was in a higher dimension where linear time is irrelevant" (p. 238). She said, "There are different dimensions, worlds existing within worlds . . . and to go from one to the next is like a roller coaster. You need to speed up the energy, and then you go to another dimension where the reality is different. In the transition from one reality to another, you feel like you're contracting and expanding at the same time" (p. 242). She "experiences the abduction encounters as important sources of 'information,' emanating from dimensions beyond or outside of physical reality" (p. 253).

Distortion of body image

In most OBEs, subjects perceive their astral bodies as being identical to their physical bodies in form and feel. However, there are several documented cases where the subject's body image is distorted. For instance, the subject may perceive the astral body as spherical, or no more than a tiny pinpoint of consciousness. Since the astral body can change into any shape, such as that of a wolf, these types of OBE may be the basis for myths and legends of human shape-shifting such as lycanthropy (werewolves), vampires, and the like. Alien abductees can also contain these properties.

Examples:

Joe's "own form kept changing, 'like a chameleon.' He felt 'more comfortable in a shape like them . . . somewhat translucent'" (p. 174). Mack also wrote that "etherical," "fluid," and a sense of "vastness" were other ways Joe described what it felt like to be in the alien form (p. 174).

Calm, peaceful feeling or ecstasy

During OBEs, it's not uncommon for the subject to describe a sense of peace, calmness, or tranquillity. This is more frequently associated with OBEs occurring within near-death experiences. There are similarities in abduction cases.

Examples:

Peter "wondered why he did not feel afraid as he is generally scared of heights" (p. 291). Arthur said, "There was absolutely no fear. In fact it was the exact opposite. It was complete euphoria, that is the only way to describe it" (p. 370).

Ability to see without glasses or contact lenses; ability to see through solid matter

During OBEs, people who would normally wear glasses or contact lenses are able to see without the aid of such devices. OBE subjects also report seeing through walls into the next room. Alien abductees can also see sometimes without the use of eyewear and/or through physical objects.

Examples:

Subject Catherine "remarkably, could see adequately throughout the experience, whereas without her lenses 'everything would basically have been a big blur'" (p. 143). Arthur recalled "seeing his family" in the car "as if the car were a convertible and he could look down on them into a car without a roof" (p. 370).

The Features of Alien Abductions According to Mack

Now that we've examined the features of an OBE, the next step is to examine the features of alien abductions and make the reverse comparison. In chapter 16 of *Abduction*, John Mack discusses, among other things, some of the common features of alien abductions. I have extracted phrases (pp. 390–92) and present them here in tabular format:

Mack's Abduction Features

No.	Common Features of Alien Abductions
1.	"Shift in consciousness" (p. 390)
2.	"Hum or other odd sound" (p. 390)
3.	"Appearance of a light for which no usual source can be found" (p. 390)
4.	"Sense of a presence or even the sight of one or more alien beings" (p. 390)
5.	"A strong vibratory sensation in the body" (p. 390)
6.	"Always sure that they are not dreaming or imagining" (p. 390)
7.	"Experience that they have moved into another reality. This is a waking reality, but a different one" (p. 390).
8.	"Taken by some force, often a beam of light or some other energy at the disposal of the alien beings" (p. 390).
9.	"Through walls, doors, or closed windows" (p. 390)
10.	"See their home and the earth itself recede before them as they are transported into a spacecraft" (p. 390)

11. "Once inside the craft the abductees see varying numbers of alien beings" (p. 390)

12. "Telepathic communications of various sorts" (p. 391)

13. "Various procedures administered under the control of a slightly taller and older-appearing alien, spoken of by abductees as the doctor or leader" (Mack describes the variety of procedures that can have a medical or surgical-like quality.) (p. 391)

14. "In some cases a person is known to have been missing, can recall, with or without hypnosis, an abduction experience" (p. 392)

15. In some cases "has returned with bodily lesions for which there seems to be no other explanation. But in other situations, 'complete' abduction does not appear to occur" (p. 392).

16. "The individual may have an out-of-body experience while others see that he or she has not left the house" (p. 392).

Interestingly, except for the references to spacecraft, bodily lesions, and medical procedures, the features of alien abductions given by Mack also appear in the list of features common to OBEs. It is also interesting to note that not all OBEs have the same features described. Typically, an OBE will contain a subset of the features described. For instance, a subject may experience vibrations in his or her body, but not see any strange lights. Likewise, alien abductions also show a subset of the typical features.

So What Are the Differences?

Physical evidence

OBEs do not generally leave burn marks on your front lawn, or scars, scoop marks, or implants.

Independent eyewitnesses

Budd Hopkins has documented cases in which multiple independent witnesses claim to have seen alien abductions as they were taking place. OBEs almost always seem to be subjectively experienced while an outside observer would describe the subject's body as "asleep."

Pain during an OBE is uncommon, but sometimes experienced in abductions

During many alien abduction experiences, subjects seem to have been subjected to painful procedures. This is almost unheard of in OBE literature. OBEs are typically painless, and have sometimes been used as a release from painful situations, as in the case of war prisoners undergoing torture.

OBEs can be consciously induced

Some subjects have been able to induce out-of-body experiences at will. I'm not an alien abduction expert, but to the best of my knowledge, alien abductions cannot be induced. If someone knows about cases where it can be, it deserves further study.

Surgeries or genetic experiments

Many cases of alien abduction seem to hinge on genetic experiments or surgeries being conducted by the aliens. Abductees report eggs being taken, fetuses being extracted, and sperm samples being collected by the aliens for some kind of genetic manipulation. Sometimes, this is described as sexual in nature, but typically it is described as being done more objectively or scientifically than that. As far as I know, people who have OBEs never report such things. It would be interesting to study whether male abductees report the termination of alien genetic experiments after a vasectomy is performed.

Degree of control

OBE experiencers usually have more control than abductees. For example, during an OBE, if subjects want to float down the hallway, they typically can do so. During alien abductions, subjects often feel out of control, and often paralyzed. For example, if they are lying upon what seems to be an examination table, they may not be able to get up.

Conclusions and Theories

A correlation?

When we closely examine the symptoms of the typical out-of-body experience and compare those symptoms with those of a typical alien abduction, the similarities are astounding. However, based on physical evidence, it's not reasonable to conclude that all alien abductions are OBEs in disguise, nor that all OBEs are alien abductions in disguise. However, the similarities are strong enough to suggest that perhaps a fair number of alien abductions have been incorrectly reported as OBEs, and that a fair number of OBEs have been incorrectly reported as alien abductions.

By the most conservative means, it is estimated that out-of-body experiences occur in approximately 11 percent to 25 percent of the population,[25] but some authors have estimated the incidence to be much higher. According to the United States Census Bureau, in 1999 the population of the United States was 272.9 million. That would mean that approximately 30 million to 68 million Americans have had an OBE. In *Abduction*, Mack states:

> Polls of the prevalence of the UFO abduction phenomenon in the United States, including a survey of nearly six thousand Americans conducted by the Roper Organization between July and September 1991 (Hopkins, Jacobs, and Westrum 1991) suggest that from several hundred thousand to several million Americans may have had abduction or abduction-related experiences.

In reading *Abduction*, I was struck by the fact that several of the alien abduction narratives contained

---

[25] Hart's 1954 surveys of 155 students at Duke University found that 27.1 percent had an OBE. Palmer's 1974 survey of 300 students and 700 adult residents in Virginia found that 25 percent of the students and 14 percent of the residents had OBEs. Blackmore's 1984 survey of 593 people from the city of Bristol, England, found that 12.2 percent had OBEs. Myers' 1983 study of a student population found that 23 percent had OBEs. Multiple surveys are summarized by Gabbard and Twemlow in *With the Eyes of the Mind: An Empirical Analysis of Out-of-Body States* (pp. 8–13).

references to out-of-body experiences. On the one hand, the descriptions of OBEs by abductees may indicate the experiences may somehow be related. On the other hand, if OBEs do occur in 25 percent of the population in general, we might expect to find OBE descriptions in 25 percent of the abduction cases. The fact that the subjects can call one experience an "OBE," and another an "alien abduction" may indicate that the subjects can somehow differentiate between the two. Since the degree of consciousness during an OBE can be equal to (or superior to) normal waking consciousness, it's difficult to determine how the subject can make this distinction. It seems worthwhile for someone to study what criteria the subjects are using to distinguish between the two experiences. It also seems worthwhile for someone to study whether alien abductees are more prone to having OBEs than the rest of the population.

A new method of space exploration?

Let us assume for a moment that out-of-body experiences are what they say they are, stepping outside the physical body to explore, without the limitations of a physical body, another dimension beyond the physical one. If such an ability were mastered, the OBE subject might be able to explore the universe, possibly including trips to other solar systems, other planets, and so forth. Subjects report that OBE travel can occur as fast as or faster than the speed of light. If this were true, given Einstein's theory of relativity, it would be far easier to explore time and space while out of body than it would be to physically move your body across solar systems. Some people have speculated that scientists of the future may one day use

OBEs as a method of studying the farthest reaches of space. If it's possible for us, it's possible for extraterrestrials as well.

Many scientists now admit that life may exist on other planets. Recent scientific discoveries related to the meteors of Mars seem to lend credence to these admissions. The problem is not whether alien civilizations exist, but whether they can span the vast reaches of space to visit our planet, one that must seem a mere speck of dust in the vast cosmos. If alien civilizations do exist on other planets, perhaps they could be using OBE as a method of exploring the universe, and learning about other physical civilizations—such as ours—through out-of-body travel. What would be the benefit? First, there could be enormous scientific gain because they could learn from technologies developed across the galaxies. They could study us for their own sciences of sociology, biology, medicine, physics, or whatever—they could improve their knowledge and technology by observing ours.

One theory that explains alien abductions is that the aliens cause the subjects to leave their bodies, inducing an OBE either through technology, telepathy, or other means, but what purpose would aliens have in studying our souls rather than our physical bodies? This seems to contradict the common claim that genetic material is being collected during alien abductions for some kind of intergalactic breeding program.

Scientists from other worlds may very well be visiting our planet and studying our civilization. The question remains whether this exploration is being done physically, nonphysically, or both.

Bridging the gap

Perhaps our universe is one multidimensional continuum of existence. Given that, it's conceivable that extraterrestrials may have learned to navigate and manipulate matter and energy between the different dimensions or planes of existence. Alien abductions are just one indication that these other dimensions exist, and that the aliens may be able to transport us, physically or nonphysically, to and from these other dimensions. At the same time, out-of-body experiences may show us that we also have the ability to navigate and manipulate the same matter and energy between the same dimensions or planes of existence, but on our own terms. Perhaps the UFO and out-of-body groups are taking two different approaches to the same thing: exploration of our multidimensional universe. The abductees see themselves as recipients, observers, or victims, while the astral travelers are explorers, proactively charting a course for humanity's own explorations of the universe. John Mack, Budd Hopkins, and a few other researchers are helping us bridge the gap between out-of-body experiences and alien abductions. I encourage both UFO and OBE groups to continue their research and bring it all together into a greater understanding of our universe.

Regardless of what out-of-body experiences and alien abduction experiences are, they both can have a profound and lasting impact psychologically as well as spiritually. It is well worth our time to further investigate both types of experience and the correlations between the two.

25

OUT-OF-BODY EXPERIENCES
VERSUS LUCID DREAMS

"Physical life is the lucid dream of the soul."
—Inner Voice

Whenever someone finds out about my interest in out-of-body experiences, the first question is usually "How do you know that it's not just a dream?"

The question is a valid one, because it has direct bearing on how seriously we should treat OBEs. While it's true that dreams can be very valuable experiences and filled with enlightening information, lessons, and subconscious messages, it's also true that, for the most part, dreams are hallucinations. If OBEs are merely hallucinations, then perhaps they have less value than some people want to believe. After all, it's easier to dismiss hallucinations as products of the physical brain, and less likely to involve any kind of immortal soul that might transcend physical death. If, on the other hand, OBEs are not hallucinations, then it may have important implications for our souls.

So are out-of-body experiences different from dreams? If you're talking about "ordinary run-of-the-mill dreams," then the answer is yes, they are quite different. For one thing, OBEs are conscious experiences, whereas ordinary dreams are unconscious experiences.

There is another type of dream called lucid dreams, where the dreamer is conscious. A more pertinent question to ask is, are OBEs and lucid dreams the same experience? To answer that question, we must first be aware of the semantics. A lot depends on how you define dreams and OBEs. If you define an out-of-body experience as an experience where your body image doesn't correspond with your physical body, then all ordinary dreams would qualify by that definition. And similarly, if you define a lucid dream as an experience of being conscious while your body is in sleep paralysis, then lucid dreams and OBEs would once again fall into the same category. If you define a dream as any experience incurred while the body is asleep, then OBEs would fit into that category. Clearly, it's important to get our definitions straight. So what is the "right" definition of a dream? The *American Heritage Dictionary* defines a dream as "a series of images, ideas, and emotions occurring in certain stages of sleep."

Suppose for a minute that my soul does leave my body and has experiences of an objective world or astral plane during an OBE. If that's the case, and I experience a series of images at that time, would it be considered a dream? Doesn't it fit the definition given above? What makes it a dream? Is it because it occurs during "certain stages of sleep?" Perhaps we need to examine the definition of "sleep" first. Again I quote from the *American Heritage Dictionary*:

> **sleep** (slēp) *n.* **1. a.** A natural, periodically recurring physiological state of rest, characterized by

relative physical and nervous inactivity, uncon-sciousness, and lessened responsiveness to external stimuli. **b.** A period of this form of rest. **c.** A similar condition of inactivity, such as unconsciousness, dormancy, hibernation, or death.

Since lucid dreamers are conscious during the experience, I could argue that lucid dreams don't occur during sleep, since they don't fit the "unconsciousness" part of the definition. Yet it seems absurd to say that lucid dreams are not dreams. To complicate matters, there are degrees of consciousness/lucidity in everyday experience. Sometimes we're more conscious and other times we're more groggy. (You should see me in the morning before that first cup of coffee!) Perhaps our definitions of dreams and sleep are too restrictive. Maybe we need to make finer distinctions of sleep experiences. Rather than bundle our conscious experi-ences into rigid categories, it's probably more accurate to define a continuum of consciousness where waking, OBEs, dreams, and lucid dreams all fit somewhere on the same scale, as I suggested in chapter 19.

So how should we label our sleep experiences? Should we label our experiences based on the strength or quality of our consciousness during the experience? Or on how "real" the scenery seems? Or should we label them on some subjective value such as how real it "seemed" or "felt?" In *Beyond the Body* (1982), Susan Blackmore defines an OBE as "an experience in which one seems to perceive the world from a location out-side the physical body." She is also quick to point out, "The *experience* of being out of the body is not equiva-lent to the *fact* of being out."

If you say that dreams are "experiences," then where do you draw the line? In my opinion, the answer lies in the definition of "hallucination." Once more I quote from the *American Heritage Dictionary*:

> **hallucination** (hə-loōʹsə-nāʹ-shən) *n.* **1. a.** False or distorted perception of objects or events with a compelling sense of their reality, usually as a product of mental disorder or as a response to a drug. **b.** The complex of material so perceived. **2.** A false or mistaken idea; delusion.

The key words are "false perception." I believe dreams are hallucinations (i.e., false perceptions) whereas out-of-body experiences are not. The scenery is "artificial" in a lucid dream, but is "real" in an OBE. I'm not trying to assert that the world we are perceiving during an OBE is the same physical world we see when we're awake. I believe that the OBE "world" is an objective reality, one that can be experienced by others (who are also having OBEs). Although the OBE world sometimes appears similar to the physical world, it doesn't always reflect what's happening there.

More Real Than a Dream

What are the differences between lucid dreams and OBEs? Once again, I turn to psychologists Gabbard and Twemlow. Chapter 6 of *With the Eyes of the Mind: An Empirical Analysis of Out-of-Body States* compares OBEs with lucid dreams. The chapter is titled "More Real Than a Dream" and contains the following table:

Comparison of Lucid Dreams and OBEs

LUCID DREAM	OBE
A. 50%–70% incidence in general population.	14%–25% incidence in general population.
B. Occurs only during sleep.	Occurs usually when awake.
C. Dreamer can consciously program the dream.	OBEer is a passive, objective observer.
D. Dreamer and physical body are still integrated.	OBEer perceives himself as separated from his physical body, which is inert and thoughtless.
E. Consciousness often vivid, with mystical qualities in experienced subjects.	Consciousness more ordinary, like being awake, even in experienced subjects.
F. Dream is seen as a totally personal (subjective) production of the dreamer's mind.	OBEer does not see it as a subjective personal production, but rather as objective reality.
G. EEG; REM dream type with occasional alpha.[26]	No typical REM findings on EEG.
H. Physical body not visible.	Physical body usually visible.
I. Fewer have a lasting positive impact.	Usually a highly positive lasting impact.

(Gabbard and Twemlow 1984)

---

[26]EEG is short for electroencephalogram, a device that measures brain waves (electrical activity at the surface of the brain). REM is short for rapid eye movements, which characterize the stage of sleep in which dreams occur.

Differences between Lucid Dreams and OBEs

The most recognized expert in the study of lucid dreams is Stephen LaBerge, Ph.D. His 1985 book, *Lucid Dreaming,* is the authoritative textbook on the subject. According to LaBerge, lucid dreams have been classified into two categories: (1) those that occur during REM sleep, also known as Dream-Induced Lucid Dreams (DILDs); and (2) those that occur during non-REM (NREM) sleep, also known as Wake-Induced Lucid Dreams (WILDs) (Levitan and LaBerge 1991). Although the data is lacking, studies on OBEs indicate they do not occur during REM sleep (Tart 1968). In fact, OBEs are typically initiated from a waking state.

With lucid dreams, the dreamer is aware of occupying the dream body, and is not aware of another (physical) body. A lucid dreamer may "realize" they have a body that's sleeping, but they have no awareness of that sleeping body. An OBEer also occupies a nonphysical body, but often is aware of their physical body in relation to where their consciousness is located. The astral body and the physical body are two different objects. Often OBEers will see their physical body, but lucid dreamers typically do not.

There are some more differences between OBEs and lucid dreams that were not part of Gabbard and Twemlow's chart, although some of these issues are discussed in their book.

- In a lucid dream, one does not typically dream about being in one's bedroom, as is common in OBEs. Also, after a lucid dream, the subject accepts the "unreality" of the lucid dream after awakening (LaBerge

1985, p. 235). After an OBE, the subject usually asserts emphatically that the experience was "real."

- Many lucid dreams contain sexual content; in fact, Patricia Garfield indicates that "fully two-thirds" (LaBerge 1985) of her lucid dreams have sexual content. During lucid dreams, sexuality is convincingly real. In other words, it feels the same as real sex.[27] OBEs, however, rarely have sexual content. When subjects report having "astral sex," the experience is not like physical sex. It's more like an ecstatic mind trip, a transfer of energy, or euphoria, but it doesn't feel like physical sex.[28]

- Lucid dreams are not easily remembered, without conditioning. LaBerge indicates that memory is a key factor of having lucid dreams. OBEs, however, are usually remembered vividly for years.

- People don't unexpectedly pass into a lucid dream from a waking state, whereas OBEs *can* unexpectedly occur from a waking state. Several people (myself included) have reported OBEs in which they have unexpectedly "fallen out of their body" from full waking conscious-

---

[27] LaBerge covers this topic well (LaBerge 1985, pp. 89–95).
[28] Monroe described astral sex as a "momentary flash of the sex charge" (Monroe 1977, p. 197), a "giddy electrical-type shock" (p. 199) and so forth. OBE veteran Marcel Forhan, a.k.a "Yram," described sensations of melting into his partner, intense vibrations, and a giddiness (Yram 1969, p. 207). Benjamin Walker states, "Sexuality only remotely reflects what will be experienced when two discarnate lovers embrace in the next world" (Walker 1974, p. 146).

ness. Some of these occurred while the physical body was active, such as walking down the street.

Also, an out-of-body experience is a typical feature of a near-death experience (NDE). One can hardly think that lucid dreams occur during an NDE, especially because the physical body doesn't spontaneously go into REM sleep during an NDE.

Occultists believe that ordinary dreams are merely out-of-body experiences, where our memories and experiences are obscured by a lack of consciousness. This theory is supported by numerous reports of "shared" or "mutual" dreams.[29] Perhaps a shared dream is an experience in the objective astral world that is obscured by the lack of consciousness.

Regardless of what OBEs and lucid dreams are, I believe they are two separate phenomena, and I'm not alone in this belief (as supported by Gabbard and Twemlow[30] and others). I do believe that occasionally people confuse one experience for the other, and granted, it's very difficult to tell the difference in some cases. One thing is for sure: more study is needed. It is premature to jump to the conclusion that "OBEs are actually variant interpretations of lucid dreams" as proposed by LaBerge.

---

[29] For examples of shared dreams, see the book *Dreamgates* by Robert Moss.

[30] "The important point here is that such phenomena are not synonymous with depersonalization, autoscopy, or psychosis, nor are they the same as dreams, twilight states, or daydreams" (Gabbard and Twemlow 1984, p. 119).

26

KEYS FOR INDUCING AN OBE

"What is love?" I asked my inner voice.
"Love is God's greatest gift to humankind:
   Himself/Herself."

When people ask me about my primary OBE induction technique, they invariably focus on the actions, visualizations, process, but not the *key* factors. They ask me why they are still unsuccessful at producing an OBE, despite hours of doing intense visualizations, concentrations, and relaxation techniques. In many cases, the reason for failure is that they are focusing on *doing* the techniques, following the instructions, instead of on using their mind properly and on taking the proper mental steps for the experience. There are five key factors that are important to inducing an OBE: state of mind, realism, motion, receptivity, and passivity.

I was delighted to find a chapter by Michael Grosso in Charles Tart's book, *Body Mind Spirit,* in which he makes a similar list called "Factors in Psi Studies

Conducive to Spirituality." In fact, Grosso's chapter fits perfectly with everything I know about inducing OBEs, so in this chapter, I'd like to draw out some of the similarities between my findings and Grosso's, as well as with a few other authors. Although Grosso's chapter dealt with the development of psi abilities in general (plus other topics), I'm going to examine what he wrote in terms of how it relates to out-of-body experiences.

State of Mind

When you are trying to leave your body, the most important thing is your state of mind. The ideal state of mind is quiet, passive, single-minded, and neither emotional nor analytical. This corresponds to what Grosso calls "Internal Attention States: The Royal Road to the Superconscious" (p. 108). He observes: "People are more likely to be receptive to the nonlocal universe if they attend to their internal states. External states distract us from awareness of ESP 'signals.'" He stresses the importance of inwardness in psychic development, then he takes it a step further by citing various religious authorities who support this idea, such as Christianity's St. Augustine and yoga meditation's Patanjali.

The point is that when it comes to inducing out-of-body experiences, it's important to withdraw your attention from the outside world and to completely ignore all sensory inputs coming from your physical body. It's equally important to turn your attention inward, accepting inputs only from nonphysical sources.

Realism

Grosso states: "Goal-oriented mental processes are not linear but imagistic; you focus on the image, the end-state." I stress that it's important to focus to such a degree that it all becomes real. It might be helpful here to examine what happens when you fall asleep. When you fall asleep, you become absorbed so deeply in your inner fantasies that you temporarily accept the dream world as reality. You feel the same range of emotions—sometimes even more intensely—than you do in waking life. To induce an OBE, you must absorb yourself into "other-world awareness" to that same degree. The gateway to the out-of-body experience is through visualizing the images and learning to focus on them to the point of realism. You have to redirect your mind to that inner space, but instead of directing your attention to the inner fantasy of a dream (a flight of imagination), direct your attention to the out-of-body state.

I'll admit that, at first glance, it might seem like self-deception. After all, you're purposely trying to use your mind to make imaginary things seem real, and that's supposed to magically transport you to another world. But all the visualizations and mind games are just mental devices to free you from your body. They are a means of tricking your mind into letting go of your body. I assure you, once you've induced your first OBE, you will see for yourself how real it is.

Motion

In my first book, I talked about the importance of motion ("swaying") when inducing an out-of-body experience. I use the momentum of the swaying sensation to propel myself out of my body.

Grosso made some astute observations when he spoke about "goal-directed psi"[31] as they directly relate to my comments about motion. Grosso writes: "As a goal-oriented process, psi neither calculates nor relies on information processing but comes about by concentrating on goals." How do my observations fit with Grosso's? When I speak of setting up a swaying motion in my imagination, that swaying has the wonderful attribute of perpetual motion. In other words, I can start the swaying motion (and throw in the visualizations to support that motion) and the motion is self-maintaining. Once started and sufficiently enforced, I can let go of the motion and it continues running.

People have a difficult time reconciling how I can talk about inducing OBEs by performing exercises like visualizations while simultaneously quieting my mind to the point of complete inactivity. To them, it sounds as if there is a fundamental contradiction between the action (visualizing) and the nonaction (keeping the mind still). Grosso's concept of "goal-directed psi" is the key. Since my swaying motion and the visualizations are set up in my mind to be in perpetual motion, I don't have to use my mind to maintain them. After I start the swaying

---

[31] Psi is a term used by many parapsychologists to denote paranormal abilities. Tart lists four kinds of psi abilities: telepathy (sending information from one mind to another), clairvoyance (perceiving what is out of the reach of the senses), precognition (seeing into the future), and psychokinesis (affecting the physical world with the mind [Tart 1997]). Others use the term more loosely to refer to any paranormal phenomena, including OBEs.

motion and visualizations and direct them mentally to keep running (i.e., after I set the goal), then my mind is free to stop all activity and become an observer. I stop all thought processes and watch the swaying increase until the momentum throws me out of my body.

Receptivity

Learn to make yourself receptive to whatever comes during practice. Along similar lines, Grosso mentions "spiritual trust." He reminds us that R. H. Thouless "talks of the 'gamelike' attitude of the successful psi experiment; the Eastern mystic talks about *lila*, the playful point of view." He mentions that William Braud "speaks of the need for cognitively 'labile' styles." Labile is a carefully chosen word, meaning "open to change, adaptable." In other words, it's helpful to take a "wait and see what's going to happen" attitude when practicing OBE.

Ideally, then, you should remain both passive and receptive. You should open yourself up completely to whatever new sensations find their way into your awareness. This complete openness can leave you feeling very vulnerable, and vulnerability can cause fear and worry, both of which will thwart your efforts to induce an OBE. That's why it's important to conquer your fear. After you start the swaying motion, you should wait with quiet anticipation for whatever comes.

Passivity

The more passive you are, the easier it is to enter the OBE state. Grosso supports this by writing, "As a goal-oriented process, psi neither calculates nor relies on information processing but comes about by concentrating on goals." In the case of OBE, it is accomplished by implanting the goals on the subconscious mind rather than by concentrating on them. In other words, success comes through being passive, not active. Grosso says: "You don't struggle with the 'how' or dwell on the obstacles that must be surmounted. . . . You don't worry about the informational steps that separate you from your goal." He continues: "Intention without desire—such seems to be the formula for success in the psychic world. . . . Oddly enough, in the face of miracles, a certain nonchalance seems the best attitude."

This view is summed up by Ken Eagle Feather in his book *Traveling With Power*: "Also known as 'not-doing,' this technique requires that you accept events just as they happen. No inference is made regarding origin or outcome of the event." He further states: "You disengage perception in order to engage it more clearly. By waiting to organize data, you enter wider horizons of reality."

Action ("doing") implies using your physical body, whether it's your brain (the act of thinking or feeling), or other more physical actions. For example, during OBE practice, you might be tempted to analyze what's happening to you, or wonder if you're doing something wrong, but by "waiting to organize data" ("not-doing") until after the experience (or even until you're separated from your body), you are much more likely to successfully induce an OBE. Of course, once you're out of your body, you can "do" whatever you want.

The Importance of Letting Go

Grosso invokes the well-known phrase, "Let Go and Let God." Letting go is important; in fact, the most common mistake made during OBE practice is keeping too tight of a grip on consciousness, also known as "not letting go enough." You have to let go of the physical world, while still retaining a slight and unwavering grasp on consciousness.

Nonpatterning

When letting go, it's important that you don't follow the usual "letting go" pattern that carries you into sleep at night. Most people have a deeply ingrained habit (pattern) of falling asleep the same way every night. Every night they let go of their consciousness, following the same sequence of events in the same way, resulting in sleep. While sleep is important to maintain mental health, it's also an undesirable result when you're trying to leave your body. Eagle Feather explains a technique, called nonpatterning, which involves deliberately breaking out of patterns of habit. Here are some examples of nonpatterning related to out-of-body induction:

Changing locations

People typically fall into their normal sleep habit instead of inducing an OBE because they make their OBE attempts from bed. They are unsuccessful at inducing an OBE because subconsciously they are programmed (out of habit) to fall asleep when they are in that location, just as Pavlov's dogs were conditioned to expect food when they heard a bell. Try inducing an OBE from another location, such as a couch, recliner, or a different bed.

Changing times

The same argument can be applied to the time we practice. Many people make the mistake of making their OBE attempts at their normal bedtime. Again, they are sabotaging their own efforts because subconsciously they are programmed (out of habit) to fall asleep at that time. Try inducing an OBE at other times.

To summarize, when attempting to induce out-of-body experiences, it's more important to attain the proper state of mind than it is to focus on performing the OBE induction techniques. Inducing an OBE is analogous to fishing with your mind.

When fishing, you've got to let out enough line to move your bait away from you. When inducing an OBE, you have to draw your consciousness down into a tiny thread and let yourself slip very close to the sleep state to move your awareness away from your body. When fishing, if you extend your line only enough so that it barely touches the water, then tug the line out of the water, you'll never catch a fish. Likewise with an OBE, if you extend your consciousness only enough so that it barely touches the near-sleep state, then tug yourself back to consciousness, you'll never induce an OBE.

If you just relax and let go, focusing more on your state of mind than on the technique itself, you will get much better results. Aiming for that quiet, passive, single-minded, receptive state of mind is much more important than any preparation or actions you take during OBE practice.

27

USING DESIRE TO ACHIEVE OUT-OF-BODY EXPERIENCES

"What is love?" I asked my inner voice.
"What is not love?"

Affirmations are powerful messages to your subconscious. Your subconscious is powerful and can take you out of your body on a moment's notice, but you should be careful with the message you're sending, because your subconscious usually takes things literally.

Affirmations like "I want to have an OBE" should be avoided because they might lead you into a state of perpetually wanting instead of achieving OBEs. On the other hand, affirmations like "I can leave my body easily" might be effective, if you can talk your subconscious into believing it. Out-of-body traveling (the action) and having the ability to leave your body (the attribute) are two different things. Your subconscious is just as likely to grant you the ability without ever exercising it.

Affirmations are like adjectives and nouns, describing you and your intended attributes, but I've found that your subconscious thinks in terms of images, goals, and desires more than words. Desires, like affirmations, are messages to your subconscious, but they are like verbs in that they call out for action. They set your subconscious in motion, and your subconscious usually tries to fulfill your desires. Rather than doing OBE affirmations stating your desires, it may be much more effective to just meditate, focusing on your desire to have OBEs. Visualize yourself leaving the body, then think to yourself, "Yes, that's exactly what I want to happen." Your subconscious will pick up on the *desire* and try to fulfill it.

I recommend you use the desire meditation as a stand-alone exercise, and also as part of your favorite OBE induction technique. Here's how it fits into my OBE technique:

- First, do the relaxation exercise until you can't feel your body.

- Next, let yourself slip as close as you can without actually falling asleep. Always maintain a thread of consciousness. Quiet down your consciousness into a single, focused thread of awareness.

- Visualize any object in front of you rocking/swaying forward and backward in a repeating cycle.

- Use your desire (intention or force of will) to give your visualization perpetual motion. Once your visualization has perpetual motion, your mind is free of its responsibility.

- The next step is to stop all thought activity (I call it "quiescing the mind") and become a totally passive observer.

- Sit back and watch the swaying increase until the momentum literally throws you out of your body.

28

THE STATE OF MIND REQUIRED TO INDUCE AN OBE

"What's today's lesson?" I asked my inner voice.
"Today, try as hard as you can to just be your-
    self.
No masks. No artificial personality. Just you."

For analytical readers, I tried to analyze and quantify some of the variables of consciousness needed to achieve an OBE. I have created charts to track the various factors involved in the out-of-body separation process. These charts follow the progression of consciousness as you go from full waking consciousness to the OBE state, broken down by "milestones" along the way, as follows:

Abbreviation	Explanation
Full	Full (waking) consciousness
Relaxing	Relaxing the body until you can't feel it
F10	Body asleep/mind awake
Hypnag.	Beginning of hypnagogic imagery

Paral.	Sleep paralysis
Vibs	Vibrations are felt
Vibs Suf	Vibrations are sufficient to start the separation
Separ.	The point of separation
OBE	After separation has occurred (OBE attained)

Some people may not notice all these milestones. For example, some people may not notice the vibrations during the separation process. Likewise, not everyone will follow the process in the same order. Due to years of practice, I can get hypnagogic images within about fifteen seconds of closing my eyes, well before my body is asleep (F10).[32] The charts reflect hypnagogic images appearing much later than I usually experience them.

At each of the milestones, you may have a different state of mind. State of mind is a complex matter. There are many variables involved, such as how much emotion you feel and how much thought you are processing. In these charts, I list some variables such as relaxation, absorption, mind-noise, quantity of thoughts. Of course, this is all subjective. The variables are based upon my analyses of what happens to *my* mind when I induce OBEs. Trying to break consciousness down into variables is a lot like trying to break down the taste of bread into quantities of "sweet,"

---

[32]The term "F10" was coined by Robert Monroe to denote a state in which the mind is awake, but the body is asleep (Monroe 1985, p. 18).

"salty," "bitter," and so on. It loses something in the translation, but I've got to start somewhere. Perhaps these categories are a starting point for further research. For the purposes of this chapter, I'll use the following variables to describe the states of mind:

Variables Involved in States of Mind

Relaxation	Absorption	Mind Wander
Stare Off into Space	Inner Dialogue	Mind Noise
Single-Minded	Thoughts	Emotions

FIGURE 1

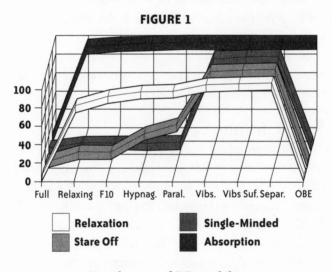

Analysis of Variables Represented in Figure 1

The numbers on the charts represent percentages from 0 to 100. For example, a "relaxation" value of 0 means I'm not relaxed at all, whereas a value of 100 means I'm completely relaxed. When the "thoughts" value is 45, I mean that I am processing and experiencing 45 percent of my normal thought content. In other words, it's a little less than half as quiet in my head than normal. These numbers are approximates. It's not always possible or meaningful to assign numbers to them, so when I say that I have 60 percent of normal emotional activity during the F10 state, that's just a rough guess. Take it with a grain of salt. The first four variables are shown in figure 1.

Relaxation

The relaxation variable is a measurement of how relaxed your body should be while you're inducing an OBE. When you begin the OBE induction technique, you should relax your body as much as possible. By the time you get to the F10 state (body asleep, mind awake) your body should be totally relaxed and remain that way until the OBE is over.

Stare Off (into Space)

The stare-off category is a subjective measurement of how passive you should be while inducing an OBE. In other words, this is how impervious you should be to stimuli, mental or otherwise. You can also interpret this as entranced if you like. Notice that the stare-off variable climbs slowly throughout the OBE induction process, and you are almost totally entranced by the time the vibrations hit you.

Single-Minded

Single-minded is a measurement of how single-minded you should be during the OBE induction process. At the beginning of the induction, you're not single-minded at all. You might be pursuing several different trains of thought at the same time. Once you get to the point where the paralysis hits, you should rapidly switch from several trains of thought to a single-minded focus on the OBE technique you're using.

Absorption

The absorption number represents how absorbed you are in what you're doing during the OBE induction process. In other words, this is how focused you are on inner events rather than what's going on outside your own mind. Try to become absorbed into inner events as soon as possible in the process. Focus your consciousness on inner events rapidly at first, and slowly build on that, until you are completely inward by the time the vibrations hit you.

Figure 2 represents the same progression of consciousness going from waking consciousness to the full OBE state, but depicts the variables not covered by figure 1.

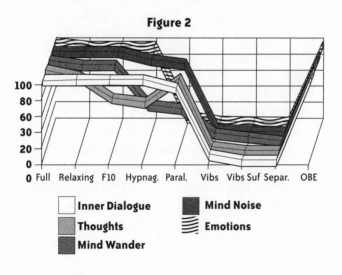

Figure 2

Analysis of Variables Represented in Figure 2

Inner Dialogue

Most people tend to mentally repeat information to themselves in a kind of inner dialogue. For example, your body may want food and give you the feeling of hunger, but most of us take that one step further by thinking "I'm hungry" to ourselves, almost like an affirmation. This happens so automatically that most people don't even realize they are doing it. The inner dialogue variable is a measurement of how many messages you say to yourself affirming that the world is how you think it is. Figure 2 indicates that during much of the OBE induction, your inner dialogue will run normally, but it needs to slow down once you reach the hypnagogic state. It should be completely stopped before the vibrations hit. Incidentally, modifying the inner dialogue messages is a very powerful tool for making changes in your life. And stopping the inner dialogue during meditation is a very powerful method of increasing your psychic awareness.

Thoughts

The thoughts variable is how much idle thinking you are doing. Is your brain running as fast as it can or are your thoughts slow to come? Perhaps this is a measurement of how "loud" your thoughts are. A value of 100 percent represents many thoughts happening often, whereas a small value indicates few thoughts occasionally. Throughout the OBE induction process, you need to continually slow down your thoughts until separation is complete.

Mind Wander

This is a measurement of how often your mind is wandering. Is it wandering from thought to thought, or is it focused on a single thought? The mind wander variable represents how often your mind switches trains of thought (frequency), whereas the single-minded variable represents how many trains of thought you have (quantity). Throughout the OBE induction process, keep your mind from wandering. By the time the vibrations hit, your mind should rapidly decrease its wandering until it is completely single-minded at the vibrational stage. With mind wander, I'm trying to measure how often you follow one thought to the next. In terms of sound, this would correspond to the frequency.

Mind Noise

Mind noise is a measurement of how distracted you are, or how often your mind switches topics. This is how much and how often you change your focus from one thing to another. Perhaps this is how fast your train of thought is running. Your mind needs to be as quiet as possible, and it needs to be totally quiet by the time the vibrations are sufficient to complete the separation from your body. With mind noise, I'm trying to measure how many new thoughts occur to you. In terms of sound, this would correspond to amplitude.

Emotions

Likewise, your emotions need to become less and less until the separation process is complete. Note that when the paralysis and/or vibrations hit you, you are likely to react emotionally. You need to calm down and refocus your mind back to the task at hand, or the vibrations will fade away and your attempt will fail. Notice also that after separation, your consciousness goes back to a near-normal state, and your thought patterns return to normal.

If you're serious about learning to induce OBEs, but nothing seems to work, this chapter is meant to help you identify what you're doing wrong. For example, maybe your mind is too noisy when you practice. I want to stress, however, that when you try to induce OBEs, you shouldn't spend all your time worrying about whether you're doing it right, nor should you spend your time analyzing what's going on in your mind. During your OBE induction, strive for that perfect, quiet, contemplative state of mind, and let it happen. Save your analysis for after your OBE attempt; then use your findings to improve upon the next OBE attempt.

29

A SIMPLIFIED TECHNIQUE FOR INDUCING AN OBE

"What's today's lesson?" I asked my inner voice.
"Today, remember that you're here on Earth to
accomplish a mission.
If you could accomplish that mission on the astral
plane, you would already be there, not here.
Don't use OBEs as an escape, but rather as a
reminder that you are a spiritual being."

Every book about OBEs should contain a chapter that explains how to do it; therefore, I provide the following simplified technique. Practice when you are not tired. For example, try it in the middle of the day, or immediately after you've slept for ten hours. This technique won't work as well if you try it right before bedtime. If possible, don't use this technique from your bed because you're conditioned to fall asleep there. If you're going to practice immediately after you've woken up, then it's okay to use your bed, as long as you haven't moved your body too much before using the technique.

Step 1: Close your eyes and relax completely.

Lie down or sit in a comfortable position and close your eyes. Relax your body completely.

Step 2: Imagine your astral body is swaying.

As you lie there relaxing, imagine that your astral body is gently rocking or swaying.

Step 3: Approach the hypnagogic state.

Let your consciousness drift down, as if falling asleep, into a near-sleep state until you see your first hypnagogic image. Let go of your hold on consciousness, just as you do when falling asleep, but be careful not to drift down too quickly, or you may fall asleep and botch the attempt.

Step 4: Wait for your third or fourth hypnagogic image.

Once in the hypnagogic state, maintain a small thread of consciousness. Watch the hypnagogic images float by until you've seen three or four of them. Be careful not to get drawn into the hypnagogic images, or you may fall asleep. Also, don't place any special significance on the images you see. Once I saw a hypnagogic image of a creature with hideous fangs that frightened me so much that I was ejected out of my body without further adieu. Once I was out of my body, I discovered that there was no monster; it had been an image created by my own mind.

Step 5: Focus your attention on a hypnagogic image.

Choose one of the hypnagogic images and focus your attention on that image. Watch and pay attention to the image to make it clearer. By focusing your attention on the image, you are taking conscious control of it.

Step 6: Stare at the image with a blank mind.

Try to empty your mind of all thoughts and feelings, and stare at the image.

Step 7: Realize the image is an astral image.

As you stare at the image, realize—without actually thinking too hard about it—that the image you are seeing is an astral image. Your *only* thought should be, "That is an astral image."

Step 8: Realize that you are near the image, and therefore you are astral, too.

Realize that you are at the same location as the hypnagogic image; therefore you are on the astral plane. Your *only* thought should be "The image is astral and I'm astral too."

Step 9: Hold that thought until the vibrations come.

Continue to stare at the image and realize your astral relationship to the image, until you feel a vibration, tingle, or buzzing sensation. Wait until the vibrations sweep into your body.

Step 10: Wait until the vibrations reach their zenith.

It may feel like you are being electrocuted, but don't be alarmed and don't panic. Remain calm, quiet, and passive until the vibrations reach their zenith and become very intense. If you try to move too soon, your attempt will fail. If you're too late in moving, the vibrations will fade away and your opportunity will be lost. You may have to experiment to learn the ideal time to wait after the vibrations hit.

Step 11: Push yourself forward.

Once the vibrations reach the peak of their intensity, you should be free to astrally push away, roll away, or sway away from your body. Now you are out of your body and free to explore.

Once again I'd like to stress that the instructions you use to induce an OBE are not as important as your state of mind and how you use it.

30

IMPROVING YOUR OBE ABILITY

"What's today's lesson?" I asked my inner voice.
"Today, feel an envelope of Love surrounding
  you,
touching everyone near you with love.
No one is ever alone."

Everyone on this planet is a spirit, but most of us
are bound too tightly to our bodies by our beliefs and
habits. We're comfortable inside our bodies, but once
we learn to overcome those beliefs, break those habits,
and start looking in the right places, *anyone* can learn
how to leave the body. It takes a lot of time, patience,
and practice. You've really got to want to get there and
devote yourself to the task, but anyone can do it.

Here are some common problems that people
encounter while trying to induce OBEs and how to
overcome them.

Falling Asleep

Since you're dealing with altered states of consciousness, it's common to fall asleep during OBE

practice. There are some easy steps you can take to avoid falling asleep:

- Practice on the couch or sitting in a comfortable chair rather than your bed.
- Practice in the morning rather than nighttime.
- Set aside a special time for OBE practice.
- If you must practice at night, go to bed an hour early so you're not tired.
- Don't listen to music while practicing.

Noises, Itches, and Distractions

It's important to maintain your focus away from your physical body while inducing OBEs. Your physical body has five senses: seeing, hearing, tasting, smelling, and touching. You can be distracted by any of these senses, and the smallest distraction seems to be magnified greatly when you're trying to keep your mind quiet. Luckily, most people don't have to worry about distracting smells and tastes during practice. Here are some tips on avoiding or getting around distractions:

Eliminate the possibility of interruptions

You don't want your practice to be interrupted. Tell others not to disturb you. Unplug the telephone. Turn off the alarm clock.

Disturbing touches

Make sure the room is comfortable, not too hot and not too cold. Put cats, dogs, and other pets in another room where they can't jump on you or disturb your practice. Wear comfortable, loose-fitting clothes, such as a sweatshirt and sweat pants.

Distracting noises

Shut the windows and turn off the television and radio. Try to eliminate as much noise as you can. If you can't cut out noises, use background noise/drone like a fan to drown out the noise. If the noise is too loud, use headphones to listen to uniform, nondistracting sounds like so-called white noise.

Visual distractions

Most parapsychologists acknowledge that psi is enhanced when distractions are reduced. For some experiments (called Ganzfeld experiments), they affix halves of ping-pong balls to the eyes of their subjects to cut out visual distractions, as well as using white noise to block out sounds.

Conditioning yourself

Through practice, you can condition yourself to become oblivious to (block out) distractions. To develop this skill, I recommend the following exercise, which requires the help of a friend you can trust. Lie down, close your eyes, and relax. After a few minutes of relaxation, have a friend tap you lightly on one of your legs or arms with his finger. Try not to flinch when you are tapped. After a random amount of time, have your friend tap you on another location. Once again, try to ignore the sensation and clear your mind. Repeat the process until you learn to ignore the sensations. As a variation, have your friend make a quiet sound rather than tapping you. Once you learn how to hold your focus without being distracted by your friend, you will be able to use this to your benefit during OBE practice.

Cut out all worrying

You'll never get anywhere if you're too busy worrying about something. Don't set time limits on your practice if it will cause you to think about how much time you have left. Don't even start to practice if you are worried about what will happen during a possible OBE. Try to resolve all these issues before you start.

If you are worried about some other problem, try to set it aside. Tell yourself that you'll have plenty of time to deal with the problem after your practice session. If that doesn't get your mind off the problem, practice at a later time when your problem is resolved.

Since we don't live in an ideal world, it's not always practical or even possible to eliminate all distractions from your practice. Luckily, you don't need to. It's still possible to induce OBEs in less-than-ideal conditions. Try a combination of the methods listed above, do the best you can, and don't get discouraged by a few distractions.

If You're Not Good at Visualization

The most common methods used to induce OBEs all seem to involve visualization, but some people are just not good at visualization.

Practice visualization

With a little practice, you can improve your ability to visualize. For example, take an ordinary object like a telephone and study it carefully. Then close your eyes and try to visualize the object just as you saw it. After a few minutes, open your eyes and examine the object again and compare the real object to your imagined object. Repeat this exercise until you can clearly imagine the object in detail. Avoid using objects with words written on them like books and magazines so that your brain's language centers don't become involved in the process.

Once you can visualize the object clearly, select another small, simple object and repeat the exercise until you can visualize that object clearly. Once you've mastered the visualization of small objects, try bigger and more complex objects. When you've got that mastered, try to visualize a whole room that you know well.

Use imagined sounds rather than sights

If you just don't work well with visual images, try imagining sounds instead. Pick a favorite song and imagine the entire song from start to finish in as much detail as possible. After you've mastered a few songs, use your imagination to conjure up various buzzing, humming, and vibrating sounds. This will sometimes cause the real out-of-body vibrations to seep slowly into your awareness.

Use imagined motion

Even if you can't create visual images or imagine sounds, you can still imagine yourself swaying or rocking, and that sensation can be instrumental in leaving your body. One way to practice this is to use a rocking chair or a waterbed to feel a genuine rocking sensation, then close your eyes and imagine the same rocking motion. Once again, you may have to repeat the genuine rocking sensation several times before you can reproduce the sensation in your imagination.

31

OVERCOMING PROBLEMS
DURING AN OBE

"What's today's lesson?" I asked my inner voice.
"Today, show your love for someone in a unique
way."

Here are some common OBE problems and how to
overcome them:

Getting Stuck to Your Body

During my early years of OBE exploration, I used
to get stuck to my body often. It was frustrating to go
through an hour-long procedure to leave my body and
then be unable to go anywhere. When this happened,
I usually struggled against it for a while, but it was useless; my astral body would just not move. Luckily, I
found a two-part solution.

Part of the problem stems from our belief systems, so
the first part of the solution is to work on your beliefs. If
you get stuck, you may be identifying with your body too
much. Your beliefs and/or fears may be holding you back.

The solution is to work with affirmations that will help you move away from your body even when it is paralyzed. For example, use this affirmation: "I can travel freely during my OBEs." This affirmation should be used throughout the day, not just when you are encountering the problem.

Part two of the solution is to properly deal with the problem whenever it arises. I've used this technique to get around the problem many times. When you find yourself stuck to your body and unable to move, tell yourself to forget the astral body, then try to push your consciousness forward, *without* the astral body. Try to leave your astral body behind. Don't try to move your astral body, try to move your mind forward instead. When you do this, your consciousness will move forward. Try to keep up the momentum until you are at least ten to fifteen feet away from your physical body.

OBE pioneer Sylvan Muldoon wrote about a "cord activity range" of ten to fifteen feet that acts like a strong gravity between you and your physical body(Muldoon and Carrington 1968, pp. 77–82). Once you are outside that range, you will be free to travel at will. Curiously, you will still have an astral body. Some researchers have described a dense semiphysical "vehicle of vitality"—like an astral body—that is related to "ectoplasm" and mediumship (Crookall 1970, p. 127). It's possible that this "vehicle of vitality" might occasionally get stuck to your physical body, and perhaps that is what gets left behind when you try to force your mind forward without the astral body.

I've also used another method to get unstuck, which is recommended by William Buhlman and Eddie Slasher: *demand* very firmly that you be released. I focused very strongly and forcefully on the thought "Freedom! Freedom! Freedom!" I repeated this until I literally felt myself pried away from my body, and I was unstuck.

Maintaining Consciousness

It's not always easy to maintain a clear state of consciousness during an OBE. If you feel yourself getting drowsy, you can try to perk yourself up the same way you would when you're feeling sleepy while inside your body. If that doesn't work, OBE expert William Buhlman, in *Adventures beyond the Body*, suggests you ask for, demand, or even scream "Clarity now!"

Problems Traveling

Most authors of OBE books made out-of-body traveling sound as easy as thinking about a place. It's not as easy as all that. When I first started having OBEs, I encountered many problems when trying to get around. Luckily, I learned to overcome these problems by doing three things:

Repairing a damaged belief system

Many of my early traveling problems were caused by flaws in my beliefs. Flying seemed unnatural and I doubted I would get to my destination. On the other hand, traveling by thought-power alone didn't make sense to me. My scientific mind was somehow convinced that it wouldn't work because there had to be more to it than that. After all, there is no room in the laws of physics for thought-based propulsion. The best way to combat these problems is by using affirmations. "When I'm a spirit, it is easy and natural to travel by thought."

Asking for help and accepting it

I never used to ask for help from spirits because I didn't trust them. Plus, I'm a guy, and guys never ask for directions! Gradually, I learned that there are plenty of spirit helpers out there who are willing to help you travel where you want to go. Once you get over the fear and distrust, you'll find out it's okay to ask for help. The residents of the astral plane are there whether you see them or not, and they can read your thoughts. To ask for help, simply think, "Can someone please help me get to . . . [state your destination]?" Most likely, you will be assisted by a helper who may be invisible and may not even speak.

Thinking yourself there

Eventually I learned how to "think" myself to another location, as described in other OBE books. The process isn't easy to explain. To travel this way, I refocus my mind on the new location, almost as if tuning my mind to a new frequency. It doesn't always work for me, so keep trying until you get it right.

Overcoming Other OBE Problems

The following OBE illustrates how to overcome OBE problems: Kathy and I were staying at Kathy's parents' house, in preparation to move to Minneapolis. Kathy left to take a certification test for a certain consulting firm. I stayed in bed to try having an OBE.

I brought my consciousness down very quickly and perfectly. I decided my best method would be to move hypnagogic images. I drifted down toward sleep, but wasn't quite there. I imagined my body was moving side to side, then I increased the movement. I didn't think I was anywhere near the right state, but I must have been because my astral body kept rattling and shaking. As I imagined stretching my astral arms out in front of me, they became real and I was suddenly, without really trying, zapped out of my body. This was about the fastest, easiest exit I've ever had.

I tried to sit up, but could only partially. I struggled to my right to get out of bed and stand up, but I was still encumbered. I tried to turn around but I was zapped back to the bed/body.

Round 2. Again, I induced the proper state with extreme ease, opened my eyes, and saw the ceiling. I thought I heard some noises as if someone were in the room, playing with the things on the little stand near the foot of the bed. I tried to listen, and finally decided to sit up to see what was there, but I had very little control. I could only sit up a foot off the bed, but not enough to see if someone was there. I tried harder until I lost consciousness and woke up in the body again. Round 3 was the same as round 2, but this time I got brave and asked, "Who's there?" No reply. I still couldn't move. I was quickly zapped back into my body.

Round 4. I got out of my body and tried to free myself again. I felt stuck, but then I felt a gentle pair of hands grab my feet and help me separate from the body. Unfortunately, I lost consciousness soon afterward and found myself back in my body again.

Round 5. I separated from my body again and decided to peel myself away from it with a backward somersault. I peeled off awkwardly, floated about three feet off the bed. I didn't see anyone. I thought about what I wanted to do next. I decided to float/fly. With that thought, I started floating up to the ceiling. Then I decided to try to visit Julia, a friend I know from the

Internet. I wanted to see if she could detect my presence, since she is psychically sensitive. I wondered how I should go about trying to get to Julia, when I received a thought-communication from an unknown invisible source who said, "It's easy. Just think yourself there."

I "thought" myself up through the ceiling and over the roof of the house. I tried to get my orientation so I could decide which direction was east. I started flying east at a great speed, perhaps as fast as an airplane, but decided "This might not work, or at least not quickly enough." The same source said, "Just think yourself there." So I thought, "With Julia." It worked! My consciousness shifted. My eyes were closed but I mind-sensed a light/energy in front of me and knew it was her. I reached my astral arms/hands out and cupped the light/energy between my hands, as if holding her head. I tried to telepath to her, "Julia, this is Bob. How are you?" Then I lost consciousness. I decided against trying for a sixth attempt.

As this journal entry illustrates, persistence is a key to solving OBE problems. If you get thrown back into your body, try to induce the OBE state again immediately, before moving your body. Do this as many times as you want. If you get stuck to your body during an OBE, try different methods to pry yourself free until you find one that works. Approach unknown entities with caution, but don't be afraid to ask for help from your spirit guides; even if you can't see them, they are there to help. If you're having problems moving to your desired destination, close your eyes and reach out mentally to your desired location, then tell yourself to be at that location by force of will.

32

QUESTIONS AND ANSWERS

"Still got questions? Look within yourself."

—Inner Voice

In my first book, I tried to answer as many OBE questions as I could imagine. Since that time, I've received OBE questions from all over the world. I will offer my opinions in no particular order.

How many OBEs have you had?

Hundreds. Possibly more than a thousand. It depends on how you count them. In many of my early OBEs, I would exit and reenter my body several times over the course of a morning. In my journals, I only counted it as one OBE when, in fact, there were several. Ultimately, it doesn't matter how many OBEs you have. What's important is what you learn from them.

Can average people have OBEs?

Yes. In fact, most OBEs happen to normal, ordinary, average people.

Can average people learn to induce OBEs?

Yes. I wasn't born with any special gifts. I learned everything the hard way. So can you.

Are some people more likely to have OBEs than others?

I don't think that certain people are more likely to have OBEs than others. OBEs happen to people of all ages, religions, races, cultures, and sexes. It happens to spiritual and unspiritual people alike.

If people can leave their bodies, why isn't it more common?

Actually, it is common. Conservative estimates indicate that OBEs happen to 25% of the population.

Can you die during an OBE or because of an OBE?

Nobody can possibly rule out the possibility of dying during an OBE, because obviously if anyone has died during an OBE, they haven't been around to warn us; therefore, all we can do is speculate. I think we all chose to come to this Earth for a purpose, and we're not going to die until that purpose is fulfilled; therefore, I don't think it's possible to die before our appointed time. If you die during an OBE, it would only be because it was your time to die, and the OBE would not have changed the timetable of your death.

In my experience, no matter how long you want to stay "out," your body will automatically suck you back in when it needs attention. So I don't even think you can commit suicide by trying to remain outside your body.

Can two people switch bodies during mutual OBEs?

If both people agree, it might be possible. We can only speculate until it's been tried. My guess is that, even if it were possible, it wouldn't be a permanent switch. You probably couldn't control the other person's body for very long. It would probably be like traditional mediumship.

Outside of fictional books, movies, and television, I've only heard of two accounts of people who may have actually switched bodies. The first case was Vincent Turvey's account of his controlling a spirit medium's body during a séance (Turvey 1969, pp. 205–11). He supposedly had signed testimonials to this feat.

The second account was from Robert Monroe, who may have temporarily entered the body of a strange man. In an OBE account dated March 11, 1961, he wrote: "I thought I had made a normal return to the physical. I opened my eyes, and was in a strange bed. A strange woman was beside the bed, and she smiled as she saw me awaken. An older woman stood beside her . . . They helped me get out of bed . . . and I knew for sure I wasn't the person they thought I was. I tried to tell them this, but they only humored me and seemed to think I was still in some sort of delirium" (Monroe 1977, p. 160).

What are the factors that encourage OBEs?

The most important factor is the amount of time and energy you spend studying and practicing the techniques and how much time you dedicate to it.

What am I doing wrong during OBE practice?

Since I can't be inside your head during practice, I can't tell you what you're doing wrong. Most beginners make the same mistakes: They try too hard, and don't let go enough. In other words, they don't let themselves slip close enough to the unconscious state; they remain too "awake."

Should I attempt OBE with my eyes open or closed?

Your eyes should be closed when practicing OBE.

How important is chakra development to OBE?

When I developed my ability, I did not do any chakra work directly. At the time, I didn't much believe in chakras. However, these days I've decided that chakras are real, since mine have been noticeably very active. Chakra development is probably time well spent, but I learned to leave the body without it, so it's not mandatory.

Why am I suddenly jolted awake when falling asleep? Does it have anything to do with OBE?

This happens to a lot of people. I believe that we leave our bodies every night during sleep. I believe that this jolt is caused when we enter the dream state before we are ready for it. I think that this happens because our subconscious or superconscious self realizes that it's mistakenly allowed too much of our conscious personality into that dream state, so it aborts the dream sequence and causes us to awaken with a jolt.

So in a way, yes, this has something to do with OBE, but it's not abnormal or paranormal. My theory is that if you can teach/convince your subconscious "it's okay to take me with you when you go out of body," then this might lead to conscious OBEs instead of jolts.

Has it gotten any easier to travel by thought since your first book?

Most OBE books claim it's easy to travel during an OBE simply by thinking about a person or place. During my early OBEs, I tried everything I could to travel by thought, but nothing worked. I'm happy to report that eventually I figured out how to travel with a thought. It took a lot of trial and error, and it's not always accurate. Also, it's virtually impossible to explain. I just pull myself to a location.

Do your OBEs happen in real time or is time distorted?

As far as I can tell, the OBE seems to happen in real time. Although some people report experiences where they seem to be in touch with events of the past or future, it has never happened to me.

Have you ever experienced time travel during an OBE?

No.

Should I worry about hitting power lines during OBE?

I haven't hit any power lines, so I'm not sure.

How do you prove that OBE is real?

Believe me, I'd like as much as anyone to prove that OBE is real. Many people have suggested that I try to fly to their house and describe some object in a particular room. There are several problems with these kinds of experiments. I tried to explain some of these in chapter 21.

If it helps, there are some OBEs reported where objective reality has been viewed and later verified. These reside in the OBE books on the market. For instance, Robert Monroe and "Miss Z" were studied by Charles Tart, and they performed some amazing OBE feats, such as reading off a random five-digit number that was hidden. The best proof is to try it yourself. That will be proof enough!

Have you ever seen extraterrestrials during an OBE?

No.

Sometimes I wake up and can't move. Is this related to OBE?

This is a well-known phenomenon called "false awakening." Many people have it, and most people are afraid of it until they understand what is happening. Basically, your mind wakes up before your body wakes up. Your mind is awake, but your body is still in the middle of the natural sleep paralysis that occurs when we all sleep. It's very difficult to break free of this paralysis, but if you do break free, either your body becomes active and you wake up, or else your body stays there, and you have an OBE. It has happened to me many times, and it's nothing to be concerned about.

What happens if you pass through a living object such as a tree?

Not much, really. Usually I get a slight shiver, but other than that, it feels the same as passing through other physical objects.

Can you manipulate matter on the astral plane and what occurs there? If so, how will this impact physical reality?

You can try to manipulate astral matter, but it won't do you much good. I've never been able to affect physical reality during my OBEs. Most of the time, your hands just pass right through the objects you see.

Can out-of-body experiences be used for wrongdoing?

I suppose OBE can possibly be used for wrongdoing, but it would be extremely difficult. Just thinking about the wrongdoing would either keep you inside your body, or else cause negative experiences.

What about privacy?

There is no such thing as privacy. Privacy is an illusion. You are always surrounded by entities, some in and some out of their body. You can inhibit them to a degree, but that's only temporary. If you are spiritual and have pure thoughts, you will not attract negative entities (they would find you boring) and you would have no secrets from anyone. I've had entities visit me while I was naked in the shower, and so forth, and it can be surprising and unnerving.

What part of us travels in an OBE?

To address this question, we have to define the soul and the mind. These are all things that can be described, but not as easily defined. If my OBEs have taught me anything, they've taught me that the soul and consciousness extend way beyond what we experience in everyday life.

I think of the part that travels out-of-body as my consciousness. I think that the astral body only exists because we are so deeply ingrained with our body image. I think that our higher self always transcends our physical body and is probably very amused by how trapped we feel inside our birdcage bodies that have a wide-open door. As someone astutely pointed out, whoever said you were in your body at all? We're just so accustomed to carrying the body around with us that we take it for granted. You can call it spirit, or soul, or whatever makes you feel comfortable, but it's all the same thing: the real you that is independent of your physical body.

Can others see you when you are in an OBE?

People who are dead or otherwise out of their bodies can usually see me. I can't always see them, but that's another topic. People who are inside their bodies never seem to see me at all. I remember one OBE where I stood in front of my wife, Kathy, trying to get her attention. Despite all my efforts, she didn't see me. Perhaps someone who can see auras could tell when I was visiting them astrally, but I've never been in a position where I could try that.

The bottom line is this: can ordinary people see ghosts? Under ordinary circumstances, no. Maybe once in a while something causes someone to see a ghost. We may be able to see someone having an OBE under those same circumstances.

What should I do if I meet a spirit for the first time?

Act the same way you would behave when you meet a stranger off the street: cautiously. Remember, spirits are just people like you and me. Some are good. Some are not so good.

Can (and should) we contact dead loved ones in an OBE?

Yes. For example, you can use astral projection to meet with and speak to your dead wife. However, I caution you that it's extremely difficult. The problem is, you are likely to be very emotional about your wife's death. It will be hard to induce the proper OBE state until you can set aside these emotions completely during the process. That's easier said than done. After you're out of your body, if you get too emotional, it can also bring you back to your body.

Are there any drugs that can induce OBEs?

Some people claim that certain drugs, such as nitrous oxide (laughing gas) or certain hallucinogens, can intermittently induce OBEs. Since drugs interfere with the brain's normal functioning, I don't trust the reality of drug-induced experiences. It's better to induce OBEs the natural way.

What else?

The twentieth century saw amazing advances in our physical reality, and with it, unprecedented materialism. My hope is that the twenty-first century will spark spiritual and psychic development on the same grand scale, and with it, a renaissance of the human spirit.

WORKS CITED

Ali, Yusef, trans., and Abdullah Yusuf Ali, trans. 1987. *The Holy Qur'an: Text, Translation, and Commentary (English-Arabic)*. Elmhurst, N.Y.: Tahrike Tarsile Qur'an.

American Heritage Dictionary, Second College Edition. Boston: Houghton Mifflin Company.

Anderson, Jon. 1983. "Horizon." On the album *Private Collection*. Polydor Ltd., Spheric B.V./Warner Bros. Music.

Blackmore, Susan J. 1982. *Beyond the Body: An Investigation of Out-of-the-Body Experiences*. London: Heineman.

———. 1992. *Beyond the Body: An Investigation of Out-of-the-Body Experiences*. Chicago: Academy Chicago Publishers.

Bradley, Marion Zimmer. 1980. *The House between the Worlds*. Garden City, N.Y.: Doubleday.

Buhlman, William. 1996. *Adventures beyond the Body: How to Experience Out-of-Body Travel*. San Francisco: HarperSan Francisco.

Burnham, Sophy. 1997. *The Ecstatic Journey: The Transforming Power of Mystical Experience*. New York: Ballantine.

Bushman, Robert. 1999. *Comprehensive OBE Bibliography*. http://www1.huskynet.com/intuitive /obe/

Charlesworth, James H., ed. 1983. *The Old Testament Pseudepigrapha.* Garden City, N.Y.: Doubleday.

Couliano, I. P. 1991. *Out of This World: Other-worldly Journeys from Gilgamesh to Albert Einstein.* Boston: Shambhala Publications.

Crookall, Robert. 1970. *Out-of-the-Body Experiences: A Fourth Analysis.* New York: University Press.

Eadie, Betty J. 1992. *Embraced by the Light.* Placerville, Calif.: Gold Leaf Press.

Eagle Feather, Ken. 1996. *Traveling with Power: The Exploration and Development of Perception.* Charlottesville, Va.: Hampton Roads Publishing.

Eckankar. http://www.eckankar.org/definition. html.

Evans-Wentz, W. Y., comp. and ed. 1960. The Tibetan Book of the Dead. New York: Oxford University Press.

Gabbard, Glen O., and Stuart W. Twemlow. 1984. *With the Eyes of the Mind: An Empirical Analysis of Out-of-Body States.* New York: Praeger Publishers.

Goldberg, Bruce. 1999. *Astral Voyages: Mastering the Art of Soul Travel.* St. Paul, MN: Llewellyn Publications.

Grosso, Michael. 1997. Chapter 5 in *Body Mind Spirit: Exploring the Parapsychology of Spirituality,* edited by Charles T. Tart. Charlottesville, Va.: Hampton Roads Publishing.

Harley, Willard F. 1986. *His Needs, Her Needs.* Old Tappan, N.J.: Fleming H. Revell Co.

Hopkins, Budd. 1997. *Witnessed: The True Story of the Brooklyn Bridge UFO Abductions.* New York: Pocket Books.

Irwin, H. J. 1985. *Flight of Mind: A Psychological Study of the Out-of-Body Experience*. Metuchen, N.J.: Scarecrow Press.

LaBerge, Stephen. 1985. *Lucid Dreaming*. New York: Ballantine Books.

Larzelere, Bob. 1982. *The Harmony of Love*. San Francisco: Context Publications.

Leva, Patricia. 1998. *Traveling the Interstate of Consciousness: A Driver's Instruction Manual: Using Hemi-Sync to Access States of Non-Ordinary Reality*. Longmont, Colo.: Q Central Publishing.

Levitan, Lynne, and Stephen LaBerge. 1991. *Other Worlds: Out-of-Body Experiences and Lucid Dreams*. Palo Alto, Calif.: The Lucidity Institute, Nightlight 3(2–3).
http://www.lucidity.com/NL32. OBEandLD. html

Mack, John E. 1995. *Abduction: Human Encounters with Aliens*. New York: Ballantine Books.

McKnight, Rosalind A. 1999. *Cosmic Journeys: My Out-of-Body Explorations with Robert A. Monroe*. Charlottesville, Va.: Hampton Roads Publishing.

McMoneagle, Joseph. 1997. *Mind Trek: Exploring Consciousness, Time, and Space Through Remote Viewing*. Charlottesville, Va.: Hampton Roads Publishing.

Megadeth. 1992. "High Speed Dirt." On *Countdown to Extinction*. Screen Gems-EMI Music, Inc./ Mustaine Music/Vulgarian Music.

Mitchell, Janet Lee. 1981. *Out-of-Body Experiences: A Handbook*. Jefferson, N.C.: McFarland & Co., Inc.

Moen, Bruce. 1997. *Voyages into the Unknown*. Charlottesville, Va.: Hampton Roads Publishing.

Monroe, Robert. 1977. *Journeys Out of the Body.* Garden City, N.Y: Anchor Press.

———. 1985. *Far Journeys.* Garden City, N.Y.: Doubleday.

———. 1994. *Ultimate Journey.* New York: Doubleday.

Moss, Robert. 1998. *Dreamgates: An Explorer's Guide to the Worlds of Soul, Imagination, and Life beyond Death.* New York: Three Rivers Press.

Muldoon, Sylvan J., and Hereward Carrington. 1968. *The Projection of the Astral Body.* London: Rider.

New English Bible, with the Apocrypha, Standard Edition. 1970. Oxford University Press/ Cambridge University Press.

O'Neill, Paul. 1993. "Edge of Thorns." From the Savatage album *Edge of Thorns.* MCA Music Corporation/Atlantic Records.

Peterson, Robert S. 1997. *Out-of-Body Experiences: How to Have Them and What to Expect.* Charlottesville, Va.: Hampton Roads Publishing.

Prabhupada, A. C. Bhaktivedanta Swami. 1970. *Easy Journey to Other Planets.* Boston: Iskon Press.

Ray, Sondra. 1976. *I Deserve Love: How Affirmations Can Guide You to Personal Fulfillment.* Millbrae, Calif.: Les Femmes.

Scholz, Tom. 1986. "My Destination." On Boston's album *Third Stage.* MCA Records/Hideaway.

Sidran Foundation. 1994. http://www.sidran.org/didbr.html

Tart, Charles T. 1968. "A Psychophysiological Study of Out-of-the-Body Experiences in a Selected Subject." *Journal of the American Society for Psychical Research.* 62(1):3–27.

————. 1994. *In Bridges to Heaven: How Well-Known Seekers Define and Deepen Their Connection With God*, edited by Jonathan Robinson. Walpole, N.H.: Stillpoint Publishing.

————. 1997. *Body Mind Spirit: Exploring the Parapsychology of Spirituality*. Charlottesville, Va.: Hampton Roads Publishing.

Taylor, Albert. 1996. *Soul Traveler: A Guide to Out-of-Body Experiences and the Wonders Beyond*. Covina, Calif.: Verity Press.

Turvey, Vincent N. 1969. *The Beginnings of Seership: Astral Projection, Clairvoyance and Prophecy*. New Hyde Park, N.Y.: University Books.

Tyson, Donald. 1997. *Scrying for Beginners: Tapping into the Supersensory Powers of Your Subconscious*. St. Paul, Minn.: Llewellyn Publications.

Walker, Benjamin. 1974. *Beyond the Body: The Human Double and the Astral Planes*. London: Routledge and Kegan Paul.

Yogananda, Paramahansa. 1971. *Autobiography of a Yogi*. Los Angeles: Self-Realization Fellowship.

————. 1995. *Bhagavad Gita: God Talks with Arjuna*. Los Angeles: Self-Realization Fellowship.

Yram [Marcel Lewis Forhan]. 1969. *Practical Astral Projection*. New York: Samuel Weiser.

INDEX

ABOUT THE AUTHOR

Robert (Bob) Peterson was born on April 14, 1961, and has been studying and inducing out-of-body experiences and psychic experiences since he graduated from high school in 1979. He graduated from the University of Minnesota Institute of Technology, with a B.S. degree in Computer Science, in 1984. While attending the university, he became more and more proficient at out-of-body exploration, while keeping detailed journals of his experiences. While at the university, he did volunteer work for a student-based organization called the Minnesota Society for Parapsychological Research (MSPR), which gave him experience as a "Ghost Buster" long before the movie made the subject popular. Bob also did editing and writing for the MSPR newsletter. Since college, he has had a very successful career in systems-level computer programming. He lived in Phoenix, Arizona, in 1985 and 1986, where he started editing and occasionally contributing articles for a local newsletter, *The Spontaneous Self*. In 1987, he moved to Rochester, Minnesota, and worked as a contract programmer at the IBM computer plant until 1996. During that time, he compiled his experiences and journals into his first book, *Out of Body Experiences: How to Have Them and What to Expect*. Today, Bob lives in the Minneapolis area with his wife, Kathy, and two dogs. His hobbies include writing, traveling, woodworking, and the game *Magic: The Gathering*.

Hampton Roads Publishing Company

. . . for the evolving human spirit

Hampton Roads Publishing Company
publishes books on a variety of subjects,
including metaphysics, health, integrative medicine,
visionary fiction, and other related topics.

For a copy of our latest catalog, call toll-free
(800) 766-8009, or send your name and address to:

Hampton Roads Publishing Company, Inc.
1125 Stoney Ridge Road
Charlottesville, VA 22902

hrpc@hrpub.com
www.hrpub.com